THE MIRACLE OF TRANSPLANTATION

The Unique Odyssey of a Pioneer Transplant Surgeon

ISBN-13: 978-1-60747-723-5

Printed in the United States of America

Phoenix Books, Inc.
9465 Wilshire Boulevard, Suite 840
Beverly Hills, CA 90212

10 9 8 7 6 5 4 3 2 1

THE MIRACLE OF TRANSPLANTATION

The Unique Odyssey
of a Pioneer
Transplant Surgeon

By John S. Najarian, M.D.

University of Minnesota
Department of Surgery
420 Delaware Street S.E., MMC 195 (mail)
516 Delaware Street S.E., 11-114 (delivery)
Minneapolis, MN 55455
najar001@umn.edu
612-625-8444 • 612-625-5420 (fax)

MEDALLION
PUBLISHING, INC.

Table of Contents

Foreword
BIG-HEARTED BOSS
by Mary E. Knatterud, Ph.D.

Big John, as this surgeon-author is often called (usually with deep affection and a dollop of irreverence), is a fitting nickname for such a gentle, influential giant. He truly has made a big name for himself in a big way as a general surgeon, transplant pioneer, and educator extraordinaire. Now in his early 80s and still working full-time in his storied Department of Surgery at the University of Minnesota in Minneapolis, he will no doubt make a big splash with this sometimes poignant, sometimes droll, and always engaging memoir.

Najarian's vigorous voice booms from every line, tempered by his unpretentious musings and wry anecdotes. Beginning in February 2007, he painstakingly crafted each chapter, 1 by 1, himself, and then dictated the text to longtime secretary Mary Dodds, after which I had the immense privilege of editing it. Beginning in February 2008, all 3 of us repeated the process, fine-tuning and filling in details as needed. His methodical surgical mind and ongoing joie de vivre made for an effective combination, incisively bringing his multilayered tale to life. This book should charm not only the worldwide community of transplant and surgical professionals but also former patients and their families, as well as nonmedical types who have long looked up to him or who would simply relish a fun, illuminating read. Equally at home with Hubert "the Happy Warrior" Humphrey and Jesse "the Body" Ventura, with fine French cuisine and State Fair junk food, and with the scientific literature and Guthrie plays, Najarian most certainly has broad appeal.

Although larger than life in surgical accomplishments and lauded by thousands of patients, trainees, and employees throughout the years, Najarian does not have a big head (at least in my admittedly biased view, after more than 2 engrossing decades of working for and with him). He has had to eat more than his share of humble pie, yet never let setbacks embitter or defeat him. I believe he has been steadied in particular by his refreshingly feisty, no-nonsense wife, Mignette Anderson Najarian, who exclaimed to me at a party during the early stages of the draft that she certainly hoped he wasn't making himself sound "too grandiose"!

One aspect of his personality that he may be too modest to shine a light on is his abundant respectfulness for others, no matter what their official position might be in this overly hierarchized world. He is the most attentive and inspiring boss I have ever had. Conscientiously mindful of everyone's time and effort, he always quickly turns around any requests for his input or approval. A trusting delegator (rather than a tormenting micromanager or a tone-deaf noncommunicator), he gave, from the outset, those of us lucky enough to be his colleagues the freedom and the autonomy to use our individual expertise in the wisest manner possible. When I started as the Department of Surgery's editor back in 1987 and met with him for the first time, I had overprepared, arming myself with voluminous notes and copious ideas for revitalizing our then-fledgling newsletter, *The Cutting Edge*: he patiently listened to me burble on for a bit, then cut me off, albeit not at all unkindly, with this succinct directive: "Just make it the best."

Yet Najarian has always been expansive with praise, once jotting me a note stating "Mary—you are a wonder! Thanks again" that made my day, and still makes my day every time I look at it. Another time, after we finished an especially arduous writing project, he surprised me with a pair of front-row tickets to a Timberwolves game that transformed my then-8-year-old twin sons' lives: perched, awestruck, on the edge of my husband's and my laps for their first-ever pro basketball contest, they became lifelong diehard fans on the spot. (When the ALG debacle sullied the headlines a few years later, my sons exclaimed in disbelief, "That would be like firing Michael Jordan for missing 1 lay-up!")

Stoic about his own problems yet unafraid to display real emotion, Najarian has always been adept at reaching out when someone else is in pain, at empathetically and meaningfully connecting. He prefers eye-to-eye communication and the personal touch to hiding behind a desk or PowerPoint slides. To share just 1 example from my own life: when my beloved mother-in-law died in January 2008, several other surgeon-friends of mine thoughtfully emailed me their condolences, but Najarian immediately jumped up from his chair and enveloped me in a big bear hug—just what the doctor ordered. I have frequently seen him in action bestowing heartfelt comfort, such as at the May 1997 funeral of Dr. Cassius Ellis, the assistant dean for minority students of the University of Minnesota Medical School and an iconoclastic director of surgical residency programs affiliated with the Department of Surgery. Najarian's big voice broke as he ended his magnificent eulogy to Ellis with this simple but profound tribute: "In my judgment, Cass was the best of his kind—humankind. I will never forget the first time he called me brother. So I'm here to say good-bye to my brother and my friend."

I have heard firsthand a continual litany of gratitude from recipients of and witnesses to Najarian's vivid caring. Two stellar instances stand out. At the January 1989 Midwinter Council meeting of the American Surgical Association (ASA) the year that Najarian was president, after-dinner speaker Walter Mondale invoked his old friend Hubert Humphrey, pointing out in a hushed tone that Najarian "was an enormous comfort to Hubert and his family in those last sad days: I saw, close up, how great surgeons work." That spring, at the April 1989 national ASA meeting, broadcast journalist Tom Brokaw stressed that "my admiration and esteem and affection for my friend, John, and his family, really know no boundaries....I have known him to be not just a talented surgeon and a generous man, but compassionate in a personal way that I will not, in fact, share with you tonight because I cherish it so much in a private way. He is a great physician and a true friend."

But whether the speeches I listened to, the interviews I conducted, and the newsletter articles I wrote featured *well*-known or *un*known beneficiaries of Najarian, they were all fervent in their admiration of his stupendous skill and huge heart.

Another dimension that may not be obvious from this memoir is Najarian's open-mindedness. He was big on affirmative action before it became a buzzword, surrounding himself with worthy residents, fellows, faculty, and staff regardless of their race, nationality, or gender. As the father of 4 football-loving sons (who once stranded their mother in a restaurant restroom, all 5 males blithely driving off in the midst of animated sports talk without realizing she wasn't with them in the car until they were halfway home), Najarian is nonetheless more feminist than perhaps he'd care to admit. Though I could never quite convince him to consistently call himself a "chair" instead of a "chairman," he once remarked in our building's elevator how pleased he was that I had kept my own unique Scandinavian surname upon marriage. He has had a positive impact on the careers of a wide range of women in our department, including just-retired nurse-administrator Barbara Elick, secretary-turned-medical librarian Sharon Kambeitz, nurse and surgical infectious disease specialist Catherine Statz, and trailblazing surgeons galore: Caliann Lum, Nancy Ascher, Sara Shumway, Melody O'Connor Allen, Jolene Kriett, Gabriela Guzman-Stein, Ginny Bumgardner, Darla Granger, Karen Brasel, Susan Congilosi, Madeline Gartner, Lucile Wrenshall, and Carolyn Cody, to cite just a few.

In short, our Department of Surgery would never have achieved what it has in the past 4-plus decades if this legendary California Golden Bear hadn't become a loyal Minnesota Golden Gopher, if this determined Rose Bowl tackle and Markle scholar hadn't transplanted himself from the West to the Midwest. Najarian's journey is instructive and intriguing: from Armenian rug merchant's son to Royal College surgeon, from 1 ruptured appendix to thousands of transplanted organs. Because of the countless lives he has saved, enhanced, and indelibly touched with his big-hearted contributions to the greater good, the world of surgery will never be the same—and the world itself is a far better place.

Preface

Now in the twilight of my career, I was urged by colleagues and students to write an autobiography about my life as a surgeon, especially a transplant surgeon. I must admit that I at first resisted this daunting task, thinking how difficult it would be to recall all of the names and dates when looking back over my career. Yet fleshing out my story turned out to be as satisfying as it was challenging: it was fun to revisit over 8 decades' worth of familial, educational, and career milestones and memories and to preserve them on paper. I have been involved with transplantation since its early clinical development to the present time. It truly represents one of the most important medical advances of the 20th century, enhancing and saving the lives of millions. I have either witnessed or participated in many key developments in this field, all while pursuing excellence in day-to-day general surgery as well. I have worked with famous surgical patients (Vice President Hubert Humphrey, pediatric liver recipient Jamie Fiske) and with thousands more, just as special, who never made the headlines.

In the over 6,000 solid-organ transplants that I have performed, I have always been amazed by and marveled at the miracle that occurs whenever I see a pale kidney graft become turgid and pink, whenever I see the first drop of urine after the graft's vasculature is connected to the recipient. That same miracle also occurs with the first sight of bile from a newly transplanted liver, with the first heartbeat from a newly transplanted heart, and with the expansion of a newly transplanted lung in a recipient who before had difficulty breathing because of congenital or acquired pulmonary disease. Thus, I felt it was appropriate to title this book *The Miracle of Transplantation.*

But in the long run, this is also an autobiography of an individual. Through many fortunate circumstances, I found myself in a position to be one of the trailblazers in this wonderful field of solid-organ transplantation. My initial course in life seemed unlikely to go in this direction, yet circumstances dictated my path. Serendipity played a strong role.

In recent years, some excellent autobiographies have been written by other pioneering transplant surgeons, among them *The Puzzle People: Memoirs of a Transplant Surgeon* by Thomas E. Starzl (University of Pittsburgh Press, 1992). Starzl carefully and accurately depicts his life's successes and failures, highlighting his education and his professional life in Colorado and in Pittsburgh. His primary goal was to make liver transplantation a success. His book teems with case histories of patients and indelible stories of the highs and lows in his monumental career.

Another compelling autobiography, *The Ultimate Gift: The Story of Britain's Premier Transplant Surgeon*, was penned by Sir Roy Calne (Headline Book Publishing, 1998). As was true of Starzl's autobiography, Calne delineates his struggles during his education to become a doctor and eventually a surgeon, followed by his own efforts to make liver transplantation a success. In addition, his other quest was to find the best possible drugs to suppress the immune response—drugs to prevent the recipient's system from rejecting the new organ. Both Calne and Starzl kept looking for the "Holy Grail" of transplantation, tissue tolerance, the ability to transplant organs without immunosuppressive drugs. To date, this Holy Grail still has not been arrived at. Intriguingly, Calne has a unique talent as an artist and painter: this hobby not only is a source of relaxation for him during holidays, but also brings to vivid life on paper many of the transplant surgeons and patients he describes in his text.

The most recent autobiography I read was *Surgery of the Soul: Reflections on a Curious Career* by Joseph Murray (Watson Publishing International, 2001). In this wonderfully written book, Murray recounts his early years in medical training and his early clinical years in kidney transplantation, for which he received a Nobel Prize in 1990. He details his true love of plastic and reconstructive surgery, which allowed him to experience the joy of repairing patients' physical disfigurement and restoring them to a more gratifying and soulful life. Murray's Christianity is very evident throughout his book.

Of several recent books for lay audiences on the history and development of transplant surgery, my favorite is *Transplant: From Myth to Reality* by Nicholas L. Tilney (Yale University Press, 2003). This very readable historical account also relates some of Tilney's own firsthand experiences as a student and then a staff member at the Peter Bent Brigham Hospital (the site of the first successful kidney transplant in 1954, between twin brothers).

To this formidable list of books by my respected longtime colleagues, I now add my own story. My unlikely beginning in life somehow set the stage for me to become one of the players in this bold field and, of greatest significance, to train over 90 transplant surgeons. If I have a legacy, I feel it would be the over 200 surgeons I've had the privilege to train, in particular those 90 transplant surgeons. I'm intensely proud of all of them and boast about them just as I do about my own 4 sons. Most of those 90 trainees have gone on from the University of Minnesota to start their own transplant programs, in this country and abroad, and to, in turn, train more transplant surgeons. My greatest professional accomplishment is thus reflected in their ongoing clinical expertise and far-flung teaching talents.

This memoir chronicles my early background and my seminal decision to follow a course of training to become a fully qualified surgeon with an emphasis on transplantation surgery. However, this autobiography would have never seen the light of day if it weren't for 3 most remarkable women. First and foremost is my wife, Mignette Najarian, who was always able to remind me of episodes in my personal life that I had forgotten, as well as correct any misconceptions that I may have had regarding dates, times, and places. In addition, she found many photographs from our personal files that made appropriate additions to the finished book. She is a brilliant partner and my best friend.

The second notable woman is my assistant, Mary Dodds, who without a doubt is the fastest typist that I have ever encountered. She would fly through my dictation, retype it, and then go over it again and again as corrections and additions were made to each page of the manuscript. In addition, she checked references for the bibliography and researched various archives of our files so that all of the names, times, and places were verified. A master of the Internet who travels the information highway with ease, she is my most important source of facts both old and new.

Last but not least is a very gifted writer and editor, Mary Knatterud. Mary edited each chapter, making sure that the words I used expressed my true feelings concerning various events in my life, personally and professionally. She made sure that the English was correct throughout and frequently suggested alternative adjectives and adverbs to avoid redundancy. I can't thank her enough for not only her editorial skills, but also her critical suggestions regarding explanations of scientific terms that would not otherwise be fully understood by lay readers.

In addition, I extend my appreciation to Bill Sullivan, executive vice president of the Institute for Basic and Applied Research in Surgery (IBARS), for his unflagging attentiveness to the well-being of our Department of Surgery and for his indispensable assistance on the publication end of this project.

This book is intended for both a medical and nonmedical audience. I hope it serves as a vehicle for providing information on the complexities and the triumphs of this wonderful field of transplantation. May every reader find these pages interesting as well as educational.

Chapter One
CAUCASUS TO CALIFORNIA

This story begins in Turkey and, more specifically, in the city of Harput. On a hill high (4,200 feet) above sea level, this ancient city was built east of the Euphrates River and next to the source of the Tigris River. On modern maps of Turkey, it can be found 4 miles northeast of the city of Elazig, which has a population of 200,000. The original city of Harput had 20,000 inhabitants, with fewer than half Armenians and the others Turks. The Harput plain is described as the most fertile in eastern Turkey. In addition, it was the center of extensive mission work and the seat of Euphrates College and Theological Seminary. After the deportation of the Armenians in 1915 by the Ottoman Turks, the old city of Harput became part of Elazig. Today, Harput (which means "rocky fortress") refers to the top of the mountain surrounded by Elazig.

My mother's family (Demirjians) lived in Harput, where her father, Toros, was a merchant selling cotton, tobacco, and wine. Eighteen years before World War I, my by-then-widowed maternal grandfather and his 6 daughters and 1 son moved to Constantinople (renamed Istanbul in 1930). Zarouhi, the third oldest of the girls, attended Constantinople College for Women, earning her bachelor of arts degree with honors in 1913. Offered a scholarship at Columbia University in New York, she emigrated to the United States with older sister Satanig and obtained her master of arts degree from Columbia on June 2, 1915. Satanig worked at Bonwit Teller, making one-of-a-kind children's dresses; sadly, she died in the World War I influenza pandemic.

Meanwhile, except for Zarouhi, the remaining members of the Demirjian family were in Constantinople when the Turks began forcing the Christian Armenians to either become Muslim or leave Turkey (1). Fortunately, because of my grandfather's wealth and government position, the family had many close ties with wealthy and influential Turks who were able to help save them from deportation or worse. One sister taught English to doctors; another became an interpreter; and my mother, Siran, was the school principal and taught English and math in high schools. So, 1 by 1, all of the family members were saved because of their vital positions in Constantinople. At the time of the Armistice (1918), American missionaries helped the family travel to Aleppo, Syria. From there they eventually obtained visas and came to the United States, settling in Boston.

Coincidentally, my father's family (Najarians) also lived in Harput, Turkey. Around 1916, 3 of them—my father, Garabed; his by-then-widowed father, Lazarus (my paternal grandfather); and my grandfather's brother Jack—left Harput and emigrated to the United States. Their sponsor was a distant relative in Fresno, California. My grandfather had been a farmer, along with Jack and their father. Jack had been handicapped because of a farming accident and subsequently became a carpet weaver, a talent that would serve him well in California, where he ultimately worked repairing oriental rugs in my father's rug store.

I vividly recall my paternal grandfather regaling us with stories of Harput. He would go to work in the cotton and tobacco fields and the grape vineyards with his father in the morning, and when the sun was directly overhead they would relax. As described by the 11th-century Persian poet-scientist Omar Khayyám in the *Rubáiyát*, they would enjoy a "a jug of wine, a loaf of bread," and cheese, followed by a short nap. As the sun fell in the west, they would return to their home, but would always first stop at the local church. It was not only a part of their religion, but also their source of information regarding events in the village and beyond. After visiting at the church with their neighbors, they would return home for their supper. This low-key and simple lifestyle probably was primarily responsible for the many centarians that lived in the Caucasus mountain region. My grandfather said that *his* grandfather lived to over 120 years of age—a statement confirmed by the family Bible, which served as a ledger of all the important family milestones, including births, deaths, and marriages.

From Fresno, my father eventually went to Los Angeles, where he enrolled in Occidental College, graduating with a degree in business. Then, with borrowed money and with the help of his father and an uncle, he started a small oriental rug store in San Francisco. It ultimately became a larger, 3-story oriental rug store on Sutter Street, between a music company called Sherman and Clay and a department store called the White House.

Once every 2 years, my father would take the train to New York City, where he would buy rugs wholesale and have them shipped back to San Francisco for sale in his store. On one of these trips, he was introduced to my mother, who still lived in Boston, but was visiting Manhattan. They had never heard of each other or their families, even though they both had originally come from the same city in Turkey, Harput. After a whirlwind courtship of just 3 to 4 days, he married my mother and brought her back to San Francisco. They eventually moved to Oakland, where I was born (the second of 3 boys). My older brother, Gerald, 2 years my senior, was the smartest of us 3. My younger brother, George, 4 years my junior, was the best athlete. We lived in an upper-middle-class neighborhood on the border of Oakland and Piedmont, California. While growing up, the 3 of us would fight—but if anyone would abuse any 1 of us, we would respond in kind to protect the victim. We were all involved in sports. We all anticipated that we would probably join our father in the rug business. The sign outside the rug store might someday read Najarian and Sons.

My interest in oriental rugs was stimulated by spending frequent Saturdays in my father's store, helping the salesmen show rugs. I was also responsible for either rolling up larger rugs on the main floor or folding the smaller rugs and stacking them on the mezzanine of our store. In addition, my father had his own private collection of fine oriental rugs, which he would take with him to women's clubs and other interested organizations, where he would present lectures on the history and the making of oriental rugs. In these lectures, he described the weaving process, the looms, the various materials used (including cotton, wool, and silk), the natural vegetable dyes, and other details. I recall with some nostalgia our

Saturday morning trips to our father's store in downtown San Francisco, while the Bay Bridge was still being built. We would drive from our house in Oakland to San Francisco Bay and board a ferry boat. On crisp mornings, we would go up to the deck of the boat as we crossed the bay and enjoy our breakfast. These enchanting trips gave us an opportunity to spend quality time with our father.

Unfortunately, our lives were altered very suddenly when my father developed an upper respiratory condition. At first, we thought it was just a simple cold. But, he had increasing difficulty breathing and his temperature rose and the doctor was called. The very day he saw him, the doctor had my father hospitalized. Two days later, he died of what was described as double pneumonia. With no antibiotics available (this was 1939), the mortality rate associated with double pneumonia was in excess of 75%. I was 12 years old. After my father's death, my paternal grandfather, who by then lived in San Francisco, continued to run the store, but given his advanced years, felt he should downsize. Still, he continued to sell rugs in a smaller store until his death at age 95 after complications from a prostatectomy.

Chapter Two
RUPTURED APPENDIX

After my father's death when I was 12 years old, very few changes took place around our home. My mother, who was from "the old country," had never driven a car. Therefore, she needed to take driving lessons in order to have a driver in the house who could provide transportation when necessary. Other than that, things (at least on the surface) changed very little because my father had always left early in the morning to go to work in downtown San Francisco, not to return until evening, 6 days a week. The only real day we ever had together as a family had been Sunday, which meant church in the morning; in the afternoon, we usually visited some of my folks' Armenian friends throughout the Bay area. Sometimes these Sunday visits were a terrible bore; but when the adults had children our age, we often found the afternoons to be very pleasant.

In the 1930s our family car was a bright red Flint that made our excursions very obvious to our neighbors and very embarrassing to us boys. Looking back, we should have been proud to be in this very unusual vehicle, which was only built from 1923 to 1927. We were embarrassed for all the wrong reasons. My 2 brothers and I wanted to blend into our neighborhood, which consisted of 4 judges, a few lawyers, and several entrepreneurs (including a family that owned a local department store). Our parents were the only ones who were obvious immigrants. Rather than embarrassed, we should have been proud that they came to this country and did succeed, fulfilling the American dream.

School progressed reasonably well. My priorities primarily involved sports, mainly football in the fall and then track and field in the spring (I was a shot-putter). In addition to sports, I was involved in student government and a prestigious boys club called the Key Club, a branch of the Kiwanis. To show we were club members, we wore a specific sweater that made us the envy of many of our classmates. I loved the Key Club colors (blue and gold) as well as its mission to develop leaders and provide vocational guidance and college scholarships. In addition to our Key Club meetings, we took it upon ourselves to become the school's "Guardian Angels": during recess and lunchtime, we would patrol the halls and grounds to prevent those people we considered "low-lifers" from smoking cigarettes on school property, which was against school rules. We acted like self-appointed vigilantes in this respect. My other activities were mostly social, including membership on a series of committees that had to do with school dances and other events.

It's interesting that the least important part of school for me was the classroom teaching. As I recall, I did just enough to get a passing grade in most classes. However, the class I enjoyed the most concerned reading selected novels, which I did at home; then, in class, I would prepare book reports. I have been an avid reader ever since. At that time, I was really not sure that algebra, geometry, history, and science would be important to me in my future life.

Then one day, just as suddenly as my father's illness hit him, I began having a stomachache that continued to increase in intensity. I felt quite sick and lost my appetite. The pain continued to progress over the next 24 to 36 hours. My mother became quite concerned and called the doctor to come and see me. Amazingly, in those days, as when my father was sick, doctors frequently made house calls. As a matter of fact, I cannot ever remember going to a doctor's office as a youngster, at any time. We always saw the doctor either in an emergency room after an accident or at home for an illness.

After the doctor examined me, he made the diagnosis of acute appendicitis. I was rushed to the hospital. It turned out that I had a ruptured appendix. Without antibiotics, the mortality rate in those days from a ruptured appendix and progressive peritonitis was quite high. The doctor who operated on me was a general practitioner who did surgery as well. Very appropriately, he opened the wound, recognized the ruptured appendix, and just left the entire wound open.

For the next 6 weeks, I lay in bed in Merritt Hospital in Oakland, the hospital I had been born in. With an open wound in the right lower quadrant of my abdomen, nurses would irrigate and clean out purulent material twice daily. The doctors would come by to see me every day to check on my progress. All of this turned out to be the best possible treatment for my condition. When the infection was over and the wound healed, I was finally discharged.

During the month and a half that I was in the hospital, I had ample time to think about my own future. I was struck by the fact that the people I admired the most were the nurses and the doctors who took care of me. Their compassion and their professionalism went beyond anything I had ever witnessed before. I felt that those nurses and doctors were very special. I recall thinking that if I came through this ordeal, I would do everything in my power to become one of them. No one in our family, either immediate or distant, was a doctor. We knew no doctors, except those who had been casual acquaintances of my parents. Therefore, I had no knowledge of how to become a doctor.

When I returned to school after my 6-week hospitalization, I went to the library and looked up every book I could find on the education necessary to become a physician. It rapidly became obvious to me that I would need a strong background in mathematics and in the physical and biological sciences. And above all, I would have to obtain the best grades possible so that I could effectively compete for admission to a medical school.

After researching everything I could find on becoming a doctor, I went to my school counselor. I told her the classes I should take in order to be admitted to the university, including English, a foreign language, physics, chemistry, and mathematics. The classes she had outlined for me included some of the softer sciences such as social studies, physical education, and 2 classes in shop (both metal and wood). I explained to her that I did not want to take those classes and kept urging her to change my curriculum to the classes I needed for the university. She insisted that I was NOT a potential university student and that I should take the curriculum she had outlined, so that I'd have something to fall back on after graduation from high school. Our disagreement resulted in a very spirited argument. Eventually, I prevailed, but not until I had made an appointment to see Mr. Ferris, the school principal, to indicate that my counselor was not allowing me to take the classes I felt I should take for university admission. I vividly remember the name of that counselor: Mrs. Schroeder. She never forgave me for going over her head to the principal to achieve my goal of preparing for university admission.

After those victories over near-fatal appendicitis and a misguided school counselor, my life course abruptly changed—academically, socially, and motivationally. In high school, I became very dedicated to attending all of my classes, doing all of my homework (and then some), and decreasing my social activities and my involvement in school council and related organizations. However, I maintained my participation in sports, both in football and in track and field.

There was never any question in my mind which university I would go to. In some ways, I had no real choice. Since my father had died, I couldn't go to Stanford, given its very high tuition and living expenses. However, I could get into the University of California, Berkeley: its tuition was only $37.50 a semester, plus I could live at home.

I had always wanted to go to Berkeley anyway, from the time I was little. Many Saturdays, when I was around 8 or 9, I took a streetcar or bus from my house to Berkeley, then sat on the side of a hill in Strawberry Canyon (the site of the Berkeley football stadium). Where I sat was called Tightwad Hill. From there, I could watch the football game. It was not the best seat in the house, but it met my financial situation. Later on (when I was around 11 or 12), with the bravado and foolishness of youth, my friends and I found ways of sneaking into the stadium. I am surprised we never got caught. It was rather challenging to scale the fence or steal past the ushers at the most opportune times—thanks to adequate misdirected diversions, particularly after the game had begun.

My interest in the University of California, Berkeley, and in football continued. When I became older, around the age of 13 or

14, I obtained a position on Saturdays selling programs and a variety of beverages at the football games. Now I could actually see the games close-up! I was also able to make a few dollars to pay for my trips from Oakland to Berkeley. Once I made the football team at Oakland High School, we football players would serve as ushers at the Berkeley games. So, throughout my precollege life, I spent my fall seasons watching every single football game that was played at the University of California. What a thrill it was, particularly in 1937 (when I was 9): that fall's outstanding team, referred to as the "Thunder Team," eventually went on to the Rose Bowl. From then on, I thought the most fulfilling dream for me would be to play for the University of California and hopefully go to the Rose Bowl.

After that fateful argument with Mrs. Schroeder, my guidance counselor, I earned excellent grades in the rigorous high school classes my principal helped me schedule. I never again was called in to see her, even though she had called me in many times before I became a dedicated student. I think she was surprised that I was doing well, since she predicted that I would not. Therefore, I made a point of saying hello to her every time I saw her in the halls—and received a slight smile in return at most. In 1945, I graduated from high school as a member of the first-string all-city football team. Along with my improved high school grades, this particular football honor had made my admission to the University of California easier.

Chapter Three
STRAWBERRY CANYON
TO THE ROSE BOWL

After graduating from high school in January of 1945, I was accepted into the University of California, Berkeley, as a pre-medical student. I vividly recall much of the first day I arrived as a freshman on campus, which I had never before explored. Most of my many previous trips to the University of California had involved the football stadium, not the campus in general. That fall, on my first full day, I approached from Telegraph Avenue and came to an impressive administrative building, Sproul Hall, and the plaza before it. Before entering campus through Sather Gate, I saw a series of card tables. They were presided over, presumably, by students, representing a variety of liberal, and to some degree, rather bizarre, causes (such as socialism, communism, and a number of Marxist theories). Generally, these students were well-behaved. Little did I realize at the time how appropriate this area was as a venue for political discussions. In years to come, among the most famous of campus activists would be Mario Savio, who rose to prominence as a leader of Berkeley's free speech movement in 1964; in fact, in 1997, the steps of Sproul Plaza were renamed the Mario Savio Steps in his honor. However, entering campus that day in 1945, the most salient thing to me was that many points of view were clearly tolerated at Berkeley, this intriguing public institution where conservative and liberal ideologies, as well as ecologic concerns, could usually be debated in a civilized and informative fashion.

After walking through Sather Gate, I was struck by the campus in general, specifically its center, which was punctuated by the campanile. Then as now, the campanile served as a symbol of the University of California, Berkeley. A beautiful park-like area with pine and fir trees caught my eye, next to the faculty club, called the faculty glade. The uppermost border of the campus was occupied by the famous Hearst Greek Theatre where graduations, Charter Day activities, memorial services, and other significant events were held, including bonfire rallies before sporting events. Further east in Strawberry Canyon, I strolled toward the familiar football stadium, then looked high up in the Berkeley hills at the world-famous cyclotron. While standing just below the stadium, I enjoyed the wonder of this beautiful campus in the Berkeley foothills, with a view toward San Francisco Bay, the bridges, and the enchanting city of San Francisco (Baghdad by the Bay, as Pulitzer-winning columnist Herb Caen dubbed it). This campus would be my home for the next 4 years, providing memories that I would cherish always.

In early 1945, on that spring day when I first arrived, the campus had been easy to negotiate, since only 5,000 students were there during the last year of World War II. Classes had been a breeze to get to and provided an inviting and comfortable feeling for an incoming freshman. However, all of that changed with the end of the war in the summer of 1945: the GI Bill enabled World War II veterans to enroll in any university of their choice. The Berkeley campus of 5,000 rapidly became quite congested with over 30,000 students. One of my larger classes in the Life Science Building had over 1,000 students in the auditorium. The instructor once asked for a show of hands as to how many students were pre-med, and half of the hands went up. He then asked how many students were pre-engineering, and the other half raised their hands. It was obvious that I was going to have to work very hard to compete with the large number of potential pre-med students now enrolled at the Berkeley campus.

There were many advantages to being at Berkeley, but one of the foremost was its reputation for academic excellence, which made it comparable to the best private universities in the United States. In 1945 when I enrolled, 3 Nobel laureates taught there; it was not unusual to take a course in physical science, chemistry, or physics and have a Nobel laureate provide a lecture. In addition, the smaller classes had a teaching assistant to give students more individual attention. By 2007, a total of 20 Nobel Prize winners had come from the University of California, Berkeley—largely due to the accomplishments of Ernest O. Lawrence, who received his Nobel Prize in 1939. His fame began in 1929, when he determined a dramatically improved method for accelerating charged particles through the equivalent of a million volts to collide with target materials, thereby creating 2 entirely new elements (i.e., neptunium and plutonium). The first cyclotron (with a diameter of 11 inches) was built in 1931; it continued to increase incrementally in size until 1942, when a 184-inch-diameter cyclotron, with a 15-foot-thick concrete shield, was completed in the most northeastern portion of Strawberry Canyon. Lawrence's brilliance and willingness to share his discoveries attracted the brightest young scientists of the times to Berkeley, many of whom went on to receive their own Nobel Prize in either chemistry or physics. On top of those 20 Nobel laureates associated with Lawrence, another 24 alumni from Berkeley have received the prize as well.

In addition to Nobel-winning achievements, the Berkeley campus is renowned for its combined libraries, which now contain over 10 million volumes. In fact, the campus library system ranks as the top public university library in the country. With diligence, hard work, and dedication, the opportunity was available to all students to achieve an education rivaling that of any private university.

On the football front, Berkeley did not have a coach in the spring of 1945. But as it turned out, earlier that same year, the San Francisco 49ers of the National Football League (NFL) had hired Buck Shaw, famed as the game's "Silver Fox," to be their first head coach starting in 1946. (Shaw had been a head coach at Santa Clara University, leading that team to win the first-ever Sugar Bowl game in 1936. Much later, in 1960, he also led the Philadelphia Eagles to the NFL championship.) So, for the 1945-46 academic year, Berkeley signed Shaw and his assistants to coach for a year while his professional team (the 49ers) was being organized. During my first year on Berkeley's football team, we played a tough schedule, which included university teams from Los Angeles, Oregon, and Washington, plus several U.S. military service teams made up of outstanding former college football players. Yet even with a primarily young group of players, we ended up with a winning season—5 wins and 5 losses. I very much enjoyed playing football in my freshman year and was pleased to be able to maintain my grades at the same time.

The following year, 1946, Frank Wickhorst was recruited from the U.S. Navy to be our coach. Unfortunately, the team did not fare well, ending up with a 2-7 season. As I look back, I feel what occurred was almost inevitable. Wickhorst had just returned from the Navy and tried to run the football team as a military operation. Most of the players, except for a few youngsters like me, were just out of the service themselves. Older and wiser, the returning veterans had seen enough time in the military that they rebelled against Wickhorst's strong discipline and almost militaristic coaching technique. Because of the unrest in the football team and the miserable season, Wickhorst was fired and his 3-year contract was paid off. As a result, Berkeley was characterized as a "coaches' graveyard." The future did not look favorable for the Golden Bears.

In 1947, everything turned around: Lynn "Pappy" Waldorf, son of a Methodist bishop, was recruited from Northwestern University to be our coach. Our Berkeley team was delighted with his selection and became even more so once we got to know Pappy. He was like everyone's friend and yet everyone's father, rolled up in one. This big jolly man obviously knew football very well. He made a point of learning all our names, even though over 100 of us were competing to make the final cut that year. It soon became apparent how much he cared about each of us as individuals. Even if I was on the second, third, or fourth team—way across the field practicing— this bellowing voice would ring out "John, keep your head up when you're making that block." He knew who all of us were, no matter how low on the roster. We each mattered to him, to the University of California, and to the football team. What a difference from the previous season! It was not long before all of us would play our hearts out for this man whom we respected, admired, and, above all, loved.

In 1947, our team was composed of many of the athletes who had played in 1946. The final roster was almost exactly the same. The only difference was a 9-1 season, rather than a 1-9 season! Our sole loss was to our archrival, the University of Southern California Trojans. A better example of the influence a coach has on a team could never be found.

Being a football player conferred many advantages. First, the professor of any given course didn't expect much. If I worked hard and did my homework, I sometimes received a better grade than I deserved. Second, from a financial point of view, no football scholarships were available at that time; however, there was a scholarship under the name of Andy Smith, the legendary Berkeley coach of the 1920s, that awarded $3,000 each year to the football player with the best grades. I won that scholarship for my second and third undergraduate years and eventually used the money that it allowed me to save for an engagement ring.

Third, another football perk was that the coaches would find on-campus part-time jobs for players so that we could make spending money as well. I enjoyed working at the lunch counter in the men's gym: even though it didn't pay much, I had a free lunch every day and could sell sandwiches to fellow football players at reduced prices under most circumstances. Even better was my Sunday job as the "guardian" of the campanile, which was only open to the public and the students that day. It was my responsibility to make sure that no one jumped off the campanile (students are supposedly prone to suicide). I was there every Sunday from 10:00 in the morning until 6:00 in the evening. Since there was nothing to do, I was able to accomplish my homework instead of spending my Sundays watching or playing sports. The only drawback was that from 4:00 to 4:30 every Sunday, one of the music professors would come up and manually play the bells in the tower, pressing down on handles attached to pullies that allowed the clappers to ring the bells. The professor would play classical music, modern tunes, and pieces appropriate for special occasions (for example, John Philip Sousa marches on the Fourth of July, "Danny Boy" near St. Patrick's Day). Students and friends throughout the campus and even some in the city of Berkeley very much enjoyed the entertainment. But after half an hour of clanging bells only a few feet overhead, I was glad when the concert was over. Incidentally, I never lost anyone, but I'm not sure I could have stopped someone who was desperate enough to try jumping off the campanile.

I finished 3 years of undergraduate studies at Berkeley in the spring of 1948, and it came time to apply for medical school. I knew this was going to be difficult, since there were only 72 positions at the campus's medical school and well over 5,000 applicants. Fortunately, I had obtained excellent grades in my 3 years by forgoing parties and almost all of the wonderful extracurricular activities that are so enjoyable in college, so that I could play football and still maintain my grades.

An important part of the application process for medical school was the interview. Two members of the medical school faculty would conduct an interview lasting anywhere from 30 minutes to an hour. I knew that my grades were good and I had the substantial extracurricular activity of football on my side, but would my interviews come off well? I was concerned because, unlike most pre-medical students, I applied to only 1 medical school, since that was all I could afford. Applying to more schools would have cost a fair amount, not only for the application fees, but also for travel expenses to the various schools for interviews.

My first interview was with a Dr. Ellen Brown, a cardiologist. It was obvious from the beginning that she was not particularly impressed by my sincerity to become a doctor. This became a difficult interview. She felt I was too young and immature, since I had only been a university student for 3 years. She thought I should spend at least another year to obtain my undergraduate degree before applying to medical school. On leaving that interview, I feared all was lost. Since I had applied to only 1 medical school, I was really depressed.

My second interview was with a Dr. George Shade, a pediatrician. He happened to be from Washington State University where he had been a running back on the football team. This interview could not have gone better. We spent most of the time talking about sports, football in particular, and I went away elated. I knew I had someone on my side.

I will always remember the day, and even the moment, that I received the letter from the medical school indicating I had been accepted. I wondered how any day could be better. It was, to me at that point, the most glorious day of my life, the fulfillment of the dream I had nurtured for so many years. My lifestyle sacrifices had paid off.

I began medical school in the fall of 1948. The first-year class was headquartered in the Life Science Building on the Berkeley campus. Since I had not taken my bachelor's degree, I had 1 more year of football eligibility left, so I could play football my first year of medical school. What a dream to have my cake and eat it too—to be in medical school and at the same time to play football at the University of California, Berkeley. Even better, I knew we were a winning team under a coach who represented one of the great role models of my life.

Medical school turned out to be just as tough as I had thought it would be. The competition was intense and required thorough attention and study. Fortunately, in 1948, our football team under Pappy Waldorf began the 2-platoon system (defense and offense). Thus, I only had to learn the defensive plays and not any of the offense. I felt I could continue in football without jeopardizing my standing in medical school. But after about 5 or 6 games, I went into Pappy's office one day and regretfully told him I had to quit, because I was getting too far behind in my studies. My fellow medical school students were in laboratories all day and would study all night. In contrast, I had to take time off in the afternoon to practice football and in the evening to go to the training table. Then I had to try to study late into the night and begin all over again the following day. This grind became more draining than I had anticipated. Pappy was kind enough to understand and wished me well in my continuing pursuit of a medical career.

Before the end of the season, however, one of the tackles was injured and I was needed back on the squad. I will never forget when Pappy called me and asked me to come back and play in the last 2 games of the season. No way in the world could I turn down this icon, Pappy Waldorf, so I returned for the last 2 games. We ended with a 10-0 season.

As it turned out, the only team in the Pacific Coast conference that we had not played was Oregon University, and they were also undefeated in conference play. The Big Ten conference selected us to go to the 1949 Rose Bowl. We were to represent the Pacific Coast conference because of our better record against the same teams. Now I faced the biggest decision of my life. Since the 1930s, I had wanted to play for the University of California, Berkeley, and to go to the Rose Bowl. I also had a strong desire to become a doctor. As Christmas vacation approached, all my medical school peers would be studying for their finals in anatomy, histology, neuroanatomy, and other subjects. If I went to the Rose Bowl, I would be spending 2 weeks in Riverside, California, practicing for the game. I thought about this for a long time, but eventually decided that I had wanted to go to the Rose Bowl long before I had wanted to be a doctor. This was a once-in-a-lifetime opportunity that I just could not pass up. So I packed a suitcase filled with my anatomy, histology, neuroanatomy, and other medical books and took them to Riverside.

We had a wonderful time in Riverside. In addition to preparing for the Rose Bowl game, we were bused to Los Angeles and Hollywood for sightseeing, including tours of movie studios. Further, the Rose Bowl had just been expanded from 90,000 to 100,000 seats, and the game would be the first nationally televised program of any sort, given the just-completed coaxial cable from coast to coast.

We played Northwestern, the Big Ten champion that year. Two sad things happened. First, I never opened the suitcase filled with all my medical books that I had so carefully packed with every intention of preparing for my finals. Second, we lost the Rose Bowl game 20 to 14. In actuality, we won the game, yet the score did not reflect it. The next day, a *Los Angeles Times* article proclaimed "How to Win the Game Without the Ball." A picture taken by the *Times* photographer showed the fullback from Northwestern, Art Murakowski, carrying the ball toward the goal line. The photo undeniably proved that a Cal player had stripped the ball from the fullback: the ball was in the air and Murakowski had not yet crossed the goal line. The official ruled that he *had* crossed the goal line *with* the ball, which the newspaper photo refuted. We had, in fact, recovered the ball in the end zone. The official's erroneous ruling gave Northwestern 7 points, including the conversion, and the score became 20 to 14. Had there been instant replay to show that the fullback did not have the ball when he crossed the goal line, we would have won the game 14 to 13. Thus, the time for instant replay had come even 6 decades ago.

Nonetheless, my childhood goal had been reached: I had started as a first-string defensive tackle in the Rose Bowl. I was able to play with Jackie Jensen, my closest friend and teammate all the way through high school and the last 3 years in college. I will never forget how Jackie and I sat and talked in the locker room before the Rose Bowl. We thought back to our days at Oakland High School. As high school football players, we never thought we would be at the Rose Bowl with 100,000 people in attendance and the entire nation able to watch on television. Jackie reached another of his goals when he became an All-American. (He went on to play professional baseball with the New York Yankees and the Boston Red Sox, and was voted the American League's Most Valuable Player in 1958.) I too, had reached my goal of playing in the Rose Bowl and was on my way to becoming a doctor.

I learned a very important lesson that season: if you have something you want done, give it to a busy person. I have lived by that credo ever since. Because I had no time during the first half of my first year in medical school that fall to spare, I had to budget my time carefully so that I could play football and still pay attention to my medical studies. That semester, I ended up with A's in my courses and passed my finals without difficulty. But in the spring of that year—the second half of my first year in medical school—I had no extra responsibilities. I was no longer playing football, so I could put all my time into medical school. Yet, I ended up with B's rather than A's because I did not have to budget my time and could go to the occasional movie and night out with the boys for a beer.

While in medical school, one thing became crystal-clear: I wanted to become a surgeon. Surgeons could actively do something to help someone directly. This appealed to my personality. As I rotated on the various services, I was drawn to cardiovascular surgery. The cardiac surgeon at our institution at that time was a gentleman named H. Brodie Stevens, who happened to have been an end on Berkeley's 1921 unbeaten "Wonder Team." His team won 4 Pacific Coast titles and became Rose Bowl champions for 4 years under legendary coach Andy Smith, whose named scholarship I had won. I admired Stevens very much and felt I would like to follow in his footsteps.

My third-year rotation in medical school was at the San Francisco General Hospital, where one fateful night I met a young nurse named Mignette Anderson, who would eventually become my wife. I distinctly remember being in a large multi-bed open ward finishing a patient workup when someone came running into the ward from the solarium shouting that her husband was choking. Mignette, who was taking care of all of the 60 patients on this ward, ran out to the solarium to see what she could do to help. Even though I was only a medical student, I felt that I should follow her in case there was anything that I might be able to do. I observed Mignette doing something with remarkable efficiency. She raised the man's arms above his head and pounded him on the back, and lo and behold, a piece of turkey he had been eating was ejected. Her action was very effective (and well before the Heimlich maneuver, popularized in 1974). On the way back to the ward desk, I told Mignette, "you were right; he was choking on a piece of food." She insists to this day that *that* was the only time I have ever said she was right.

I don't know if there is such a thing as love at first sight, but I realized that night that I needed to get to know Mignette better and proceeded to ask her out for a date. Since she always worked the night shift, I would wait until she was off and then drive her home; I guess that was what we called a date. She was not only gorgeous, but also unique. From the small town of Benson, Minnesota, she was a farmer's daughter who helped him with the farm and helped her Swedish mother around the house and also assisted in the raising of her 4 sisters and 1 brother. She was educated in a one-room schoolhouse. When I met her, Mignette and her roommate, who also came from Minnesota to California, were living together in a small apartment in the Mission district. It was her roommate's idea that the 2 of them would come to California and work just long enough to make enough money to continue their planned trip around the world. Their next stop would either be Hawaii or somewhere in Asia, and then they would continue on from there. Luckily, I was able to persuade Mignette to stop in California and hopefully I would be able to take her to see the rest of the world.

The following fall, her parents came out to San Francisco for a visit. In her apartment, I did as she had requested: I got down on 1 knee and asked her father for permission to marry her. He agreed. In my fourth year of medical school, I went back to her hometown of Benson, where we were married in Trinity Lutheran Church on April 27, 1952. As a slightly dark-complected Californian, I stood in the front of that church filled with her relatives and friends, all Scandinavians and a few Germans and all staring at this unfamiliar-appearing stranger from the West Coast. It seemed like forever before her father brought her down the aisle. Her 4 sisters were the bridesmaids and her brother was the best man. Unusual for April in Minnesota, the temperature was near 95 degrees. There was no question that I was sweating this one out. However, this was undoubtedly the most important day of my life. No one could have found a better or more supportive partner in life than I did.

The only people at the wedding besides her family and friends were my mother and my mother's 4 sisters, all staying with my aunt Zarouhi, who now lived in St. Paul, Minnesota. Mignette's and my honeymoon consisted of driving back to California with my mother and her sister Haigouhi. This made for an interesting honeymoon trip home! On returning to San Francisco, I completed my fourth year of medical school and graduated in June 1952. I passed my board examinations and was fortunate enough to be selected as 1 of 6 straight surgical interns at the University of California, San Francisco.

Chapter Four
THE IMPORTANCE OF 1954

After I graduated from medical school and successfully completed California's State Board Examinations, I promptly began my surgical internship at the University of California Hospital in San Francisco on July 1, 1952. In preparation for my internship, I secured a single-room apartment (with a Murphy bed) about 2 blocks from the hospital. I knew that I would need to be near the hospital, considering my duties as an intern. Little was I prepared for what was to come.

The chances of my ever getting home were slim to almost none. Our day as surgical interns usually began at 5:30 in the morning, and it was rare that we completed our duties before 11:00 p.m. or midnight. We put in close to an 18-hour day, 7 days a week. Every third weekend, we were given the luxury of a day and a half off. Often, I was so tired that I would just sleep in the interns' quarters at the hospital rather than go home, even though it was only 2 blocks away. On top of patient care and operating room time, I did much of the lab work for my own patients, as did my fellow interns. For example, we performed blood crossmatching tests the day before patients' operative procedures.

Currently, interns and residents in the United States are legally allowed to work only an 80-hour week, in stark contrast to the more than 120 hours a week that my fellow interns and I worked in the 1950s. To my knowledge, there was no problem with patient care despite our long hours. In many ways, in fact, I feel we provided better patient care because we were so continuously responsible for our own patients 24 hours a day: at least 18 hours in the hospital and on call at home as well.

Our chief of surgery at that time was Dr. H. Glenn Bell, who had trained at the University of Cincinnati Medical Center under one of the brightest surgeons trained by Dr. William Halsted, namely Dr.

Mont Reid. I therefore felt that we were third-generation Halsted trainees. Neurosurgeon Dr. Howard Naffziger, who was the chief of surgery at the University of California Hospital in the 1930s, had recruited Bell to assume the chairmanship of the Department of Surgery in the early 1930s. Bell was a superb general surgeon, and over and above that, an outstanding human being. It was always a pleasure to scrub with him: the procedure was often almost bloodless, as he followed the gentle, meticulous surgical techniques introduced by Halsted. Every Sunday morning, Bell insisted on making walking rounds. Beginning at 8:00 a.m., we would start our rounds and go through all of the general surgical services, then have our noon lunch together in the hospital cafeteria. And every New Year's Day, Bell hosted an informal breakfast party at his house for all of us surgical interns and residents—one of the highlights of the holiday season. I occasionally wondered whether he had these breakfasts on New Year's Day to see who might have overcelebrated New Year's Eve.

On the third weekend (when we had half of Saturday and all of Sunday off), we occasionally participated in an operation on Saturday morning that went beyond noon. Of course, we could not leave until the operation was completed. In this respect, the one service that we dreaded the most was neurosurgery, since the chief of neurosurgery was one of the most overly meticulous surgeons I had ever seen. It was not unusual for him to spend 14 to 18 hours removing a hemangioma (a tumor composed mainly of blood vessels) from the brain. Unfortunately, on one of my supposedly half-Saturdays off, I was on the neurosurgery service and we didn't complete the operation on which I was assisting until almost 2:00 a.m. on Sunday. My job that day and night was to use the sucker to remove the blood and smoke from the operative field as the vessels were individually resected and coagulated. That experience helped convince me that neurosurgery was not the field for me. The saving grace was that the operating rooms on the third floor of the hospital had windows to the outside. Thus, even when we were totally bored by a procedure, as I was by neurosurgery, we could look out and see Fort Miley (the location of the San Francisco Veterans Hospital) and, further out, the Pacific Ocean. Although the view made our experience tolerable, it was also depressing to realize that the sun was shining and we were confined to the operating rooms.

When I did have my day and a half off, Mignette and I celebrated with a fine dinner. It frequently consisted of horse meat, which we could buy for 27 cents a pound, or a large bowl of spaghetti, followed by a half gallon of Gallo wine, which I believe cost less than $1.00. After this sumptuous meal, we usually ended up going to a drive-in theater to see a movie. Frankly, most often, I fell asleep, which made me a less than exciting companion.

As my internship wound down, those of us who had not already spent time in the military entered the service of our choice, since the Korean War was raging. We each were required to complete 2 years of military training. I chose the Air Force, following in the footsteps of my older brother, Gerald, who had been a tail gunner in a B-17 during the latter years of World War II. After 6 weeks in boot camp in Alabama, I was assigned to be a division surgeon in Albuquerque, New Mexico, on Kirtland Air Force Base, beginning in August 1953. My position, division surgeon for the 34th air division defense, meant that I was responsible for 3 bases, all of which were early aircraft control and warning (AC&W) sites. I also oversaw the medical care at Davis-Monthan Air Force Base in Tucson, Arizona. I traveled to these 3 AC&W bases by car and conducted medical rounds. The medical technicians at each base saved the complicated medical problems for me to see on my visit every 2 to 3 weeks.

Back at Kirtland in Albuquerque, I helped out in the local infirmary. Fortunately, we were right across the street from the Lovelace Clinic, established by Dr. William Randolph Lovelace, a surgeon from the staff at the Mayo Clinic in Rochester, Minnesota. His nephew, Dr. Randy Lovelace, was one of the designers of the BLB oxygen mask (the L for Lovelace, the first B for American medical researcher Walter Meredith Boothby, the last B for Turkish-born American medical researcher Arthur H. Bulbulian). Mignette obtained a position at the Lovelace Clinic as a surgical nurse working for Randy Lovelace. Whenever I could take some time off,

I went to Bataan Memorial Hospital next to the clinic where the doctors from the Lovelace Clinic operated and helped in the operating room. The elder Lovelace was used to the Mayo Clinic style of surgery, in which a surgeon would begin a surgical case in one operating room and then the primary surgeon would come in and perform the essential part of the operation and leave, after which a surgeon in training would come in and close. While the primary surgeon was in the first room, another case would begin in an adjacent room, so in this manner, the primary surgeon could be responsible for 2 operating rooms at the same time. As it turned out, Mignette and I were the 2 people who would open as well as close for Lovelace. We had an ample amount of time in the operating room and, I must say, Mignette was a great technical surgeon.

My military service turned out to be a wonderful break for us, because it was our only real time to be together since our wedding. During my internship, we hardly saw each other, except on those very brief occasions when I would have a day and a half off. Of my memories from my time in the service, the most vivid occurred when I first arrived at Kirtland, thanks to the high altitude of Albuquerque (about 5,000 feet). The first time I was the on-duty surgeon at the infirmary, a jet airplane crashed on takeoff. The pilot apparently had been able to eject and was possibly alive, so I jumped in an ambulance and went to the crash site. The pilot had indeed successfully ejected: we finally spotted him at least 100 yards from the crash site. I started running toward him to see if I could do anything to help. By the time I got there, since I was not yet acclimatized to the altitude, I was extremely short of breath. I wondered if I was the one who would need medical help, rather than the Marine who had just ejected himself from his jet. To our amazement, when I arrived, he was in fairly good condition, still strapped in the pilot seat. Other than a possible broken arm, he was okay. Talk about a tough Marine!

My main goal from my medical school years and throughout my surgical internship was to pursue a career in cardiac surgery, so I spent time in the medical library on Kirtland, as well as the one at Bataan Memorial Hospital. One day I read an article by

Dr. F. John Lewis from the University of Minnesota, published in 1953 in the journal *Surgery*, stating that he had operated on several individuals with small defects in the atrial septum (the wall that divides the 2 nonpumping upper chambers of the heart). Lewis described how the patient's body temperature was lowered to 28 degrees centigrade; the chest would then be opened, and all venous inflow to the heart would be stopped for 5 to 6 minutes while the surgeons closed an opening of 2 centimeters in the atrial septum. The first such patient, a 5-year-old girl, recovered uneventfully. This represented the first open-heart operation under direct vision. By 1954, Lewis had performed open-heart surgery to correct atrial septal defects in 11 patients using hypothermia. Only 2 patients died during the operation and 2 others thereafter. Lewis's series was a major breakthrough, but with only 5 to 6 minutes to work with, the use of hypothermia had definite limitations for most cardiac surgery.

I then read an article in the *Journal of Thoracic Surgery* in 1954, in which Dr. C. Walton Lillehei's group at the University of Minnesota described controlled cross-circulation for open intracardiac surgery. One dog provided oxygenated blood for a recipient dog. The femoral vessels of the donor dog were cannulated, and the blood was pumped directly into the blood vessels of the recipient dog. These operations in dogs allowed the surgeons over 30 minutes with a bloodless heart, enough time to correct most intracardiac lesions. In March 1954, Lillehei and his group applied this technique of cross-circulation to human patients. The first recipient was a 1-year-old boy with a hole in his interventricular septum (the wall separating the 2 pumping chambers of the heart). His father served as the cross-circulation donor. The boy's septal defect was easily closed under direct vision.

At that time, I had friends in the surgical residency at the University of Minnesota who advised me that Dr. Richard A. DeWall, a University of Minnesota graduate, had developed a simplified bubble oxygenator that was successfully used in experimental trials of some 70 dogs in 1954. By 1955, Lillehei felt that the DeWall oxygenator would be ready for human patients.

Thus, while in the Air Force, I became aware that further progress in cardiac surgery would quickly continue, with better pumps and better oxygenators on the near horizon. I realized that future progress in cardiac surgery would come through advances in technical engineering. Clearly, the DeWall oxygenator heralded the beginning of more sophisticated heart-lung machines that would allow the ever-increasing numbers of cardiac surgeons to correct almost all complicated congenital heart defects.

At the end of 1954, the news of a medical breakthrough on December 23 hit the newspapers and radio: a successful identical-twin kidney transplant had been performed at the Peter Bent Brigham Hospital in Boston. The operation was performed by a young plastic surgeon on the Brigham staff, Dr. Joseph E. Murray, who worked in the experimental laboratory perfecting techniques for kidney transplantation. The surgeon in charge of the experimental clinical transplant service, Dr. David M. Hume, had transplanted kidneys from deceased donors into the thighs of 9 human patients in renal failure, with 1 kidney graft functioning for 6 months. However, Hume was called to serve in the Korean War, so Murray became the surgeon for both experimental and clinical transplantation at the Brigham Hospital. It was quite appropriate that Murray performed the first kidney transplant with long-term success, since the technique used (placing the graft in the right iliac fossa, with connections to the iliac artery and vein) was the one that he had developed in dogs in the laboratory. This technique of kidney transplantation in the iliopelvic position was similar to the technique described by Dr. René Küss of France in 1951 (2). It is the same technique that we continue to use at the present time, over a half-century later. Of course, with identical twins as the kidney donor and recipient, there is no genetic difference between the 2, since they are derived from a single egg; thus, it was possible to successfully transplant an organ such as a kidney between identical twins without the concern of rejection. The success of that December 1954 operation proved that the technical problem of organ transplantation had been solved. Rejection in recipients without an identical twin became the essential research focus to ensure the future of this field.

My life course abruptly changed toward the entirely new and exciting field of organ transplantation. Just imagine, I thought, if we could only overcome the immune response that results in rejection of foreign organs! It would be possible to simply replace damaged, diseased, or defective vital organs with new ones. Acceptance of foreign organs between nonidentical twins (or between other related or unrelated donor-recipient pairs) rests on controlling the immune response and sufficiently suppressing it. The goal is to allow for acceptance of a foreign solid-organ graft without endangering the recipient's natural immunity to infection.

I felt I needed to know more about immunology if I were to pursue this new field of organ transplantation. All I remembered from medical school immunology was what I had learned in microbiology, which primarily related to infectious diseases and only slightly touched on the basics of the immunologic response. Therefore, during my upcoming surgical residency, I vowed to myself that I would learn as much as possible about immunology and that, on completion of my residency, I would find a mentor who would provide an opportunity for me to do immunologic research. The excitement of beginning this new course of study and research in the field of immunology presented a new goal for my postresidency research. After 2 years in the Air Force, I was honorably discharged in 1955 and returned to the University of California, San Francisco, to finish my surgical residency.

Chapter Five
THE JOY OF RESEARCH

After returning in 1955 to the University of California, San Francisco (UCSF), for my surgical residency, I felt it was important to get involved as quickly as possible in research. The basic foundation of academic medicine is research. At that point in my life, I really had no bona fide experience, to speak of, in any research laboratory or in the arena of clinical research. Thus, when offered the opportunity to spend 1 year in a UCSF research laboratory (out of my 5 years of surgical residency), I immediately volunteered, along with my friend and fellow resident Dr. Dwight Murray Jr. Of the 6 individuals beginning surgical residency, only 2 would go to the laboratory; I was very fortunate to be 1 of those 2. In actuality, though, I think the other 4 had no real ambition in that direction.

The UCSF surgical research laboratory was under the directorship of Dr. Horace J. McCorkle, a professor of surgery who was responsible for maintaining the so-called "dog house." The dog house served 2 purposes. First, it provided an opportunity for residents to do surgical research. Second, it was used as a resource to teach surgical techniques to medical students. However, the surgical research mission had not been fully realized until 2 years before I arrived, with the hiring of Dr. Harold Harper, a professor of biochemistry from the nearby University of San Francisco. His part-time job was to help the surgical residents with their research projects, including the writing of research grants and papers. An outstanding biochemist, Harper was the author of a softcover textbook entitled *Review of Physiological Chemistry*. This textbook, published by Lange Medical Publications, was considered by UCSF medical students to be the best biochemistry resource, with clearer definitions and explanations of biochemical reactions than the standard recommended textbooks. We were quite pleasantly surprised to have Harper in our laboratory to help us design our experimental protocols and prepare the methodology for conducting our research.

One of my laboratory projects involved collaborating with Harper on the possible treatment of the condition known as hepatic coma, in patients with liver failure. Harper felt that, biochemically, the amino acid arginine would be an excellent way of treating the cause of hepatic coma, namely, ammonia toxicity. As it turned out, he was absolutely right. Our experimental treatment consisted of giving arginine to animals with high levels of blood ammonia; for human patients with hepatic coma, we also recommended administration of intravenous arginine. This aspect of my research was responsible for my very first medical publication, "The Effect of Intravenously Administered Amino Acids on Blood Ammonia" (3). Eventually, the project resulted in 10 of my first 17 publications.

Another project during my year in the UCSF laboratory grew from a study I had designed while at Kirtland Air Force Base in Albuquerque. This project used a food blender to create a suspension of skin particles to transplant in patients who had extensive third-degree burns but insufficient donor skin sites for autotransplants. Although I successfully grafted the skin suspension, it was not a real-world solution for burn patients, since the grafts were too thin for practical coverage (4).

A third project that I pursued in the UCSF surgical research laboratory tapped the illeocecal valve as a substitute for the cardioesophageal sphincter. With this surgical procedure, I transplanted the valve that separates the large bowel from the small bowel to the site where the esophagus meets the stomach, thereby preventing regurgitation of gastric acid into the esophagus, a condition known as GERD (gastroesophageal reflux disease) (5). GERD typically results in erosive esophagitis, so preventing it with such an operation seemed reasonable. However, the operation was quite complicated. Fortunately, a variety of sophisticated yet simpler antireflux operative procedures were developed in the mid-1950s that became the treatment of choice.

I presented each of the 3 research projects—on blood ammonia, on skin particle suspension, and on ileocecal valve transplants—at the Surgical Forum at the annual national meeting of the American College of Surgeons (ACS) in 1956. I was thrilled to have all 3 papers accepted at the prestigious Surgical Forum, a showcase for young investigators. I very much enjoyed giving these 3 presentations that October at the ACS meeting in San Francisco. I found that presenting research material to a large group of fellow surgeons was enjoyable and ego-satisfying. I then knew I could successfully perform research and persuasively report it. My career in academic surgery was well on its way.

The most important of those 3 research projects was the 1 on treating hepatic coma with arginine, because it extended to the clinical side of my residency. Actual human patients that I saw were successfully treated with arginine. I was often asked to medical meetings to speak on that subject and to discuss the use of arginine and other amino acids in the treatment of hepatic coma. To this day, this approach to ammonia toxicity is still effective. My laboratory mate, Dwight Murray, helped on many of those experiments. In addition, I assisted him with one of his research projects that he also described at the 1956 Surgical Forum regarding the absorption of radioactive iron after gastrectomy in dogs (6).

Our time in the UCSF research laboratory was exceedingly special. During the remaining 4 years of residency, we would return in our spare time to the laboratory to help with both new and continuing projects that involved translational (that is, bench to bedside) research. One such project, under the supervision of McCorkle, examined the effect of pancreatic secretions on the gallbladder. Our results were eventually published in the *Archives of Surgery* (7) and the *American Journal of Surgery* (8). Thus, I was beginning to be recognized as an active contributor to the field of gastrointestinal research.

As much as I loved my research time, I relished, to the same degree, the chance to give talks at surgical meetings. Since many of the talks were limited to 10 minutes, which the meeting organizers were strict about, I started out by memorizing my talks so that they would end after 9½ minutes. Although memorization was a good way of initially proceeding, it lacked spontaneity. When my confidence level rose, I was able to give my talks more naturally by simply speaking, aided only by brief notes, instead of reading or memorizing a rigidly prepared text. I think that my joy in speaking and my success in that realm was inherited from my father, who delighted in speaking to various groups about the history and significance of oriental rugs. He probably derived more pleasure from those presentations than from the more mundane aspects of merchandising. It must be a genetic thing, since all 4 of my sons have been quite successful in public speaking; 2 of them appear almost weekly on national cable (CNBC), giving pointers on managing investments, and another graduated from Berkeley in theater arts.

As I was completing my 5-year surgical residency at UCSF, I began investigating options for postgraduate training in immunology. Harper, my mentor, had some good friends in London, particularly in research. Through his efforts, I applied for a research position with 1960 Nobel laureate Peter Medawar, who said he would accept me in his laboratory. But he already had someone for the coming year, so I would have to wait at least 1 year before joining him. I made further inquiries, including to Professor Michael Woodruff in Edinburgh, Scotland, but would also have to wait at least 1 year before I could join his research laboratory.

Since my main desire was to gain immunologic knowledge, I began, with the aid of Harper, to pursue information on immunologists in the United States. One name rapidly emerged from my review: Frank Dixon, a young scientist who had recently been appointed chairman of the immunopathology department at the University of Pittsburgh's medical school. In reading about his background, I realized that this was an unusual scientist. He had worked at Harvard University with Shields Warren, a pathologist who eventually became the first chief of the division of biology and medicine at the U.S. Atomic Energy Commission (AEC). Because of Warren's connection to the AEC, Dixon had access to radioactive materials that were otherwise difficult to obtain. Dixon began applying the technique of tagging proteins with radioactive iodine. Using this technique, he could follow proteins injected into laboratory animals and confirm their location and number with a Geiger counter. After completing his pathology training at Harvard, Dixon obtained a position on the faculty at Washington University in St. Louis. He applied the new radioactive techniques that he had learned to gain a better understanding of the condition known as antigen-antibody complex serum sickness. With the tools of radioactive iodine tracers and a new technique for making proteins glow under ultraviolet light (immunofluorescence), Dixon was able to quantitatively answer many questions in immunology. Dr. Jonas Salk at Pittsburgh recognized Dixon's talents and recruited him in 1951. At 31, Dixon was named the nation's leading medical researcher under the age of 35 by the prestigious American Association for the Advancement of Science. Thus, to me, he looked like someone who really was making impressive progress in the understanding of immunology. I promptly applied for a position in his department and was accepted.

With Mignette and 2 sons, Jon and David, I left San Francisco in 1960 for Pittsburgh to embark on an immunologic career. Our trip was quite eventful. We left California in a Hudson Hornet that we had purchased from my father-in-law, who ran a Hudson dealership in Benson, Minnesota. We fixed the back seat of the Hudson Hornet so that our 2 boys could sleep there. I would try to stop during the day at a motel, where I would sleep and they could swim or take advantage of the area. Since we had made the back of the Hornet into a bed, we had most of our clothes and other belongings packed into a small Crosley automobile that we pulled behind our Hudson as a trailer. We also had an overhead rack on the Hudson that was filled with personal belongings as well.

I drove at night: since it was summer and we had no air conditioner, the heat would thus not be a problem. The most disturbing occurrence on that trip was that, somewhere in Montana, we ran out of gas. I had not been careful in my judgment as to the amount of remaining gas and forgot that, late at night, gasoline stations were not open in the small towns. My major concern was that we had passed a derelict walking down the highway at 2:30 in the morning on this deserted Montana highway. He would soon be approaching us. Worried about my young wife and 2 small sons, I attempted to siphon gas out of the Crosley, using my stethoscope tubing. This technique did not work. Mig then suggested that I disconnect the gas line to the carburetor: fortunately, her idea worked, but I wasn't fast enough. The next thing I knew, the derelict was there beside our car! He asked me for a ride, explaining that he was just out of prison and had been told he must leave the state as soon as possible. I told him that I would like to help, but as he could see, I had a major mechanical problem with the car. Luckily, he accepted my answer and continued his walk down the highway.

The next and more concerning episode occurred a few minutes later. A group of mischievous bikers came down the highway on their motorcycles. Mig was running around helping to get gas into the Hudson, and our 2 sons were running around in the back of the Hudson like a couple of chained dogs. The bikers stopped. Mig later told me that she was more uneasy about them than about the derelict who had recently passed our out-of-gas car. Here was this attractive young lady in her shorts and tank top stranded with 2 nonworking vehicles that were obviously brimful of all our worldly goods, plus 2 helpless tots. Fortunately, after a brief conversation, the bikers became uninterested in us and wished us well as they left.

When I had enough gas transferred to the Hudson to hopefully get us to the next town, I began to drive down the highway. About 2 or 3 miles later, we passed the derelict once again. He was surprised and obviously angry as he saw me go by. As we proceeded down the highway, we suddenly encountered a mountain lion—an unusual sight on the highway, since it would be there only if hungry. The mountain lion was going in the opposite direction. I was quite concerned: it was heading in the direction where the ex-con would be walking. I just hoped that everything turned out all right and that he did not end up as dinner for the mountain lion. I tried to look in the papers the next day to see if anyone had been mauled by a mountain lion in Montana. No news was good news. From that time on, I carefully made sure we always had enough gas in the car, especially if facing long distances between small towns in the middle of the night.

When we arrived in Pittsburgh, I was assigned to work in Joseph Feldman's laboratory. An outstanding immunologist and scientist, he became a good friend. Having been blessed with biochemist Harper as a mentor at UCSF, I now was lucky to have Feldman as a scientific role model for me in the field of immunology. Most of my research time in Pittsburgh was spent learning laboratory techniques, as well as learning immunology. As an added advantage, since this was the department of pathology, I also received training as a pathologist.

Feldman was interested in delayed hypersensitivity, which at that time was thought to be the immunologic process that resulted in the rejection by the host's body of foreign tissue grafts. This topic fit very well with my ambition to learn as much as I could about the immunologic response of a recipient to a foreign tissue graft. I learned the techniques of labeling cells with radioactive isotopes so that I could follow their action against a graft. In addition, I mastered immunofluorescent techniques and found out how to inject mice, rats, rabbits, and guinea pigs. Most of my time in Pittsburgh was spent on developing the tools necessary to actively pursue research projects in basic immunology.

The move to Pittsburgh also turned out to be an interesting experience for my 2 sons, Jon (age 3) and David (age 1½), since it was their first time to live in the snow. We found a small apartment in the town of Greentree, right across the river from Pittsburgh, through the Fort Pitt tunnel. From a family point of view, everything went very well in our stay in our apartment. Although our small boys enjoyed the snow, Mig frequently had to help shovel my car out so that I could go to work. That particular year, 1960, a whopping 77 inches of snow fell in Pittsburgh, extremely rare for that city. I was not prepared for that much snow. As a result, it was often impossible for me to get out whenever it had snowed a significant amount, particularly since the University of Pittsburgh medical school where I worked was on top of a hill. Still, I was usually able to negotiate the roads and didn't miss too many days of work.

My family and I took several fun and informative trips, including to Philadelphia where the boys had a chance to see the Liberty Bell, and to Washington, D.C., where they took in an equally impressive array of historical monuments. In May 1961, I went to New York to take my surgical boards, and made time to see New York City and to visit 2 of my relatives there. Since I had been out of active clinical surgery for the past 8 months, I was apprehensive about passing the surgical boards. However, I was subsequently told by my former chief of surgery, Leon Goldman in San Francisco, that he received notice of my passing my boards with the highest possible grades. I was gratified by this news and by the communication from Goldman, who also indicated that, as soon as I completed my research studies in Pittsburgh, a position awaited me on the surgical faculty at UCSF.

Meanwhile, the work of Dixon's laboratory in Pittsburgh had come to the attention of Edmund Keeney, an allergist who was running the Scripps Clinic in La Jolla, California. Keeney wanted to start a research program at the clinic and contacted Dixon to see if he could possibly recruit him to La Jolla. Unbeknownst to all of us in his laboratory, Dixon had once hitchhiked as a young man from his home in Mankato, Minnesota, to La Jolla. He found it to be one of the most beautiful areas on the west coast. As the Spanish term makes clear, it is the jewel. He felt he would love to live there some day. The offer to Dixon from Keeney would mean no more teaching duties and no medical school administration hassles. It would be pure autonomous research along with miles of beach, temperate sea air, and endless summer. The decision for Dixon was easy.

The next thing I knew, our laboratory would be moving from Pittsburgh to La Jolla as an entire group: 4 professors, 6 postdocs, and support staff. A new adventure was in the offing: living in La Jolla, working at the Scripps Clinic and now Research Foundation with the hottest immunologic group in the country at the time. Mignette and I, with our 2 boys, began our trek back to California, once again in the reliable Hudson Hornet with its large overflowing overhead rack, pulling the Crosley jammed with our clothes and other necessities. I must admit that we probably looked a lot like the Joads of *The Grapes of Wrath*. Happily, we made the trip back without any of the challenging experiences that had marked our drive from California to Pittsburgh. I never ran out of gas. Nor did we encounter any former convicts, bikers, or mountain lions.

On arriving, we found a small house in the Clairemont area of San Diego that we rented for the first 9 months or so. Eventually, we located a delightful smaller house in an area called Bird Rock in La Jolla, only 4 miles from the Scripps Clinic and Research Foundation. This house met our needs very well—it was close to work for me and close to the beaches for Mig, Jon, and David. In addition, we had the luxury of having an orange tree in our backyard, close enough to our back porch that we could pick oranges in the morning for breakfast directly off the tree. Two avocado trees served as sources for making guacamole in the early evenings when I returned home from the laboratory. All in all, the experience in San Diego and in La Jolla was lovely. Pregnant with our third son (Paul), Mig was glad to be in southern California with its beautiful ocean playgrounds and warm climate. Professionally, I had acquired in Pittsburgh the tools I needed to accomplish basic immunologic research. Despite the distractions of being in such gorgeous surroundings, I felt I could be productive during the weekdays, even though the blue-green Pacific just outside our laboratory window surely was a temptation (albeit unfulfilled) to occasionally play hooky.

Chapter Six
ANATOMY OF THE IMMUNE RESPONSE

I was quite excited as I began my research laboratory experience in La Jolla, at the Scripps Clinic and Research Foundation, in 1961. With the research tools I had acquired in Pittsburgh and with the mentorship of Dr. Joseph Feldman, I had a unique opportunity to dissect the most basic parts of the immune response. Gaining knowledge of the anatomy of immunity would allow me to really learn immunology (a). My work would also help me clearly define the roles of the molecular (b) participants in the immune response. At that time, the focus was on 3 components to an immune reaction: first, an antigen, defined as any substance that can elicit an immune response; second, an antibody, a protein that is produced in response to stimulation by an antigen; and third, complement, a group of serum (c) proteins activated by limited proteolysis (d). Complement is only present in humoral (body fluid) immunity, and not in cellular (e) immunity.

Before leaving Pittsburgh, Feldman and I conducted a series of experiments to determine the role of immune cells (f) in the tuberculin (g) reaction. The tuberculin reaction is the classic model for cellular immunity. By tagging the sensitized cells in this reaction, we were able to follow their location and function in experiments on guinea pigs. While the laboratory in La Jolla was being set up, we had an opportunity to collect and record our

---

(a) immunology—the branch of science dealing with a human's or animal's response to a foreign body, such as a transplanted organ, or to a disease-causing invading microorganism, such as a virus
(b) molecular—related to a group of 2 or more atoms comprising a particular chemical substance
(c) serum—fluid from blood or tissue
(d) proteolysis—the breakdown of proteins into peptides, amino acids, and other dissolvable substances
(e) cellular—related to a cell, the smallest independent functioning unit of an organism
(f) immune cells—lymphocytes from lymph nodes, which filter bacteria and foreign particles, and from the spleen
(g) tuberculin—a liquid containing proteins from cultures of the bacterium that causes tuberculosis

findings obtained in Pittsburgh: I submitted my first immunologic article to the *Journal of Experimental Medicine*, published by Rockefeller University Press in New York City. This publication is considered one of the most prestigious journals reporting immunologic research. Much to my amazement and delight, the paper we sent at the end of July 1961 was accepted and rapidly published 3 months later in the November issue (8). With this paper, I was on course to be accepted as an immunologist. To this day, I feel this was the most important of the 1,300 articles of mine that would ultimately be published. My research career in immunology was now off and running. The next 23 articles in my bibliography were all related to basic immunologic research.

Using the technique of radiolabeling (h) cells and determining their action in transplanted tissue with the use of autoradiographs, Feldman and I were able to achieve another 7 published articles in the *Journal of Experimental Medicine*. In my medical school days, immunology had primarily concerned infectious diseases, vaccinations, and autoimmune pathologic conditions. But now, a few short years later, I had the tools to explore the role of lymphoid cells, stem cells, and bone marrow cells, as well as their reaction to a variety of antigens and, most critically, to foreign tissue antigens. As we dissected the immune response, we confirmed the role of antigens in 2 major classifications (humoral immunity and cellular immunity). Humoral immunity was an area that Frank Dixon (my laboratory mentor in Pittsburgh and then La Jolla) pursued, using the research tools of radiolabeled proteins, Geiger counters, and immunofluorescence. His primary studies were directed at understanding antigen-antibody serum sickness, which is responsible for rheumatoid arthritis, lupus, and antigen-antibody complex disease of the kidneys.

Our studies in mice of tissue transplantation progressed. It soon became evident that transplant immunity did not follow the accepted dictum described by most investigators as cellular immunity (9). At the site of tissue rejection, we frequently could find

---

(h) radiolabeling—tagging cells with a radioactive tracer

only a few scattered radiolabeled cells that were sensitized to the tissue. It appeared as though many transplant recipients' own cells were recruited by these few sensitized cells. Therefore, our subsequent studies were more sophisticated. We transferred sensitized cells in Millipore chambers (which are impervious to cells), in an effort to determine if there was also an antibody response in transplant immunity. When we sonicated (disrupted with sound waves) the sensitized cells, we found that the resultant serum would reject foreign tissue grafts without the involvement of the sensitized cells. Thus, the immune reactions we were studying appeared now to be as in ancient Gaul, divided into 3: cellular, humoral, and transplant immunity. Today, transplant immunity is known to involve antigen-presenting cells induced by both T (thymus-derived) lymphocytes for lysis (cell destruction) and by B lymphocytes (from bone marrow) for antibody production; the reaction is amplified when the number of cytokines (secreted polypeptides) increases.

For the next year and a half (1961-1963), I was generally accepted nationwide and beyond as an immunologist. I became a member of the American Association of Immunology and made presentations at the Federation of American Societies for Experimental Biology in Atlantic City, as well as at a variety of immunology meetings throughout the United States and abroad. One of the most complimentary comments that I received came after I presented a paper to the Immunology Society. A very distinguished immunologist came up to me and said he was surprised to find that I was a surgeon; in following my presentations and publications, he had always felt I was an immunologist. I told him I was most flattered by his remark.

Besides the seminal research work being done in the laboratory, Scripps fostered a very nice collegial atmosphere among all the postgraduate fellows and the staff. We would meet each day for lunch, discussing our projects and often planning collaborative studies. In addition, we would have conferences at least once a week where we would go over the results of our research and critique one another's presentations. Another advantage was the frequent visits of scientists from all over the country, thanks to the impressive work being done by the Dixon group. These visitors included immunologists such as bone marrow transplant pioneer Dr. Robert Good from the University of Minnesota; polio vaccine developer Dr. Jonas Salk, who was moving from Pittsburgh to La Jolla to build the Salk Institute; Dr. Bernard Amos; and Dr. Rupert Billingham, who, along with Leslie Brent, informally shared the prize money for the 1960 Nobel Prize with Peter Medawar. We were able to meet with these eminent experts and talk about our research projects with them. Their advice and counsel were invaluable in critiquing our work.

During the 2½ years that I spent in Pittsburgh and at Scripps, the only formal meetings that I participated in pertained to basic science, specifically immunology—no surgical conferences. In addition to the various immunologic societies and the Association for the Advancement of Science, I also joined several less formal organizations. The one that I recall the most was the Hagfish Society, a group of immunologists who would meet occasionally to discuss recent advances in immunology. A hagfish is a type of fish that is basically a scavenger or parasite; some wags thought this described our members. So, this ignominious slimy fish ironically was a symbol of an elite society of premier immunologists. As I recall, Good was the president of this society.

From a family point of view, our year and a half in La Jolla was extremely pleasant. We dubbed our third son, Paul, born at the Sharp Memorial Hospital in San Diego, a "sharp" baby. Mignette's parents came to visit us and we had many enjoyable times together. Being so close to the Mexican border, we went to Tijuana on several occasions to see the sights and to purchase inexpensive leather goods and silver. The weather was always good; Mignette and the children very much enjoyed the beaches, the wonderful San Diego Zoo, and the availability of outdoor concerts and theater.

Professionally, after a year in Pittsburgh and then a year and a half at Scripps, I had accomplished what I had set out to do, namely, to become a knowledgeable immunologist. With continuing advances in immunology, I felt that successful organ transplantation would soon become a reality. In the meantime, Dr. Leon Goldman, the chairman of surgery, was anxious to have me back on the staff at the University of California, San Francisco (UCSF). In the early winter of 1963, I informed Dixon that I would be leaving the Scripps Clinic and Research Foundation to return to San Francisco. Dixon urged me to stay and said that I could be the chief of experimental surgery at the Scripps Clinic. I informed him that, after spending 6 years in surgical training, I wanted to return to patient care and to the practice of surgery, which I dearly loved. He understood and wished me well.

Our family now moved once again, this time a much shorter distance from La Jolla back to northern California. I was very much looking forward to organizing a program in kidney transplantation at UCSF. Only 1 other such program was then in existence in the state, at the University of California, Los Angeles (UCLA), under the directorship of Dr. Willard Goodwin, a urologist. Elsewhere in the country, kidney transplant programs had also been recently founded in Denver (by Dr. Thomas Starzl); Minneapolis (Dr. William Kelly); Richmond, Virginia (Dr. David Hume); and Boston (Dr. Joseph Murray).

Chapter Seven
MOUNT SOLEDAD TO
MOUNT PARNASSUS

In many ways, it was difficult to leave the beauty of La Jolla (the jewel), steeped in the blue-green waters of the Pacific and in the shadow of Mount Soledad, adorned with its statuesque 43-foot Easter cross. It seemed as if we were leaving paradise. However, the journey ahead was one I was anxious to complete, because after arriving at Mount Parnassus (now named Mount Sutro) on the campus of the University of California, San Francisco (UCSF), I would be able to continue my quest toward developing an eventually successful organ transplant program. This journey was shorter than the ones Mignette and I had made before with our sons. Rather than pulling the Crosley containing many of our possessions, we were now in 2 cars: a Chevy Corvair, which my father-in-law had brought with him from Minnesota, and, of course, the reliable Hudson Hornet that had taken us back and forth across the country.

After we were settled in San Francisco, I found that I would be sharing my office with another surgical faculty member, Dr. H. Glenn Bell, who had been my chief during much of my surgical residency. I would also be sharing a secretary for help with academic tasks. Our chief of surgery was Dr. Leon Goldman (the father of current U.S. Senator Dianne Feinstein), who placed me in charge of the research laboratories, a position that was previously held by Dr. Horace McCorkle when I was a surgical resident. Thus, I had an opportunity to do my research, but in addition, I also had to spend some time looking for patients, since my salary would only be augmented by income from patient care.

I devoted much of the early months on the UCSF faculty writing research grant applications to the National Institutes of Health (NIH), so that I could obtain much-needed research funds. On obtaining my first NIH research grant, I was provided with an office on the 9th floor of the Moffitt Hospital, with an adjoining research laboratory next door. This particular office and laboratory combination had been occupied by Dr. Harold Harper before he became a dean for graduate studies. It was an ideal arrangement for me.

My next goal, after establishing a patient base and securing research funds, was to begin to set up a clinical kidney transplant service. First and foremost, I needed a nephrologist who could work with me in caring for patients with renal failure awaiting a transplant; the first one I worked closely with was Dr. Frank Gotch.

To achieve a successful transplant team, I had to have a well-organized person to help coordinate our 3-pronged efforts on the clinical side (working with potential kidney donors and recipients), in the operating room, and in the laboratory. This person would be called a transplant coordinator. I recruited for this position a surgical nurse, Justine Willmert, who became the very first transplant coordinator, that I'm aware of, in the United States.

Finally, to complete our team, I had to find someone who would be willing to perform the donor operation, removing 1 of the kidneys from a living donor. This individual had to be an outstanding technical surgeon who could remove a kidney without harming either it or the donor in any way. I chose Dr. Edwin J. Wylie, the chief of our vascular surgical service and among the best technical surgeons on the UCSF faculty. I knew he would do a superb job of removing a kidney with its blood vessels and ureters intact.

While organizing our clinical transplant team, I continued to work in the surgical research laboratory with 2 colleagues. Dr. William Silen was primarily interested in gastrointestinal research; eventually, he left to assume a position as a professor of surgery at Harvard and as the chief of surgery at Beth Israel Hospital in Boston. My other laboratory colleague was Dr. Frank Moody, who was also interested in gastroenterology research; eventually, he left to take a position on the faculty at the University of Alabama. The 3 of us represented an odd group to the rest of the UCSF faculty, whose primary interest, unlike ours, was always clinical surgery. The other faculty couldn't understand why the 3 of us spent so much time in the research laboratory, rather than going out and hustling up patients to treat, thereby augmenting our income.

The dog laboratory continued to be a wonderful place for training UCSF medical students in surgical procedures; the 3 of us enjoyed helping them in this regard once a week. In addition, I tried to provide an opportunity, as McCorkle had done when I was a resident, for surgical residents to spend a year in the laboratory. And I also made the laboratory available to residents even after they returned to the clinical service.

Chief of surgery Goldman had graduated from the University of California, Berkeley, in 1926, where, like me, he competed on the football team. In 1930, he was also an Alpha Omega Alpha (AOA) graduate from the medical school (AOA is the national honor society for medical students). Goldman became the first-ever surgical resident at UCSF in July 1930. After completing his residency, he was appointed to the staff of the medical school as an instructor in surgery. In 1938, he obtained a fellowship in gastroenterologic physiology with Dr. Andrew Ivy at Northwestern University in Chicago. When he returned to the UCSF staff in 1939, it was obvious he would become an outstanding academic surgeon with a strong interest in research. Unfortunately, Goldman developed Crohn's disease and was never able to realize his full potential as a research investigator and surgeon. However, he was always admired, by the residents and the medical students alike, because of his extensive knowledge of the surgical literature and his interest in surgical research. At the end of 1963, because of his ongoing health issues, he stepped down as surgical chairman. A search ensued for his successor. Much to the joy of the faculty, residents, and students, Dr. J. Englebert Dunphy, who had been the chairman of the surgery department at the University of Oregon, became our chairman at UCSF in 1964.

Dunphy was a stellar surgeon. He had attended the College of the Holy Cross in Worchester, Massachusetts, and then Harvard Medical School, before entering surgical training at the Peter Bent Brigham Hospital in Boston. After completing his surgical training during World War II, he entered active duty in the surgical service of the 5th General Hospital under Dr. Robert Zollinger. At the end of the war, Dunphy returned to the faculty at Harvard and subsequently served as the director of the surgical service at Boston City Hospital. Dunphy was somebody that everybody in surgery revered. His appointment gave instant credibility to the program at UCSF. He had been president of almost all of the preeminent surgical societies, including the Society of University Surgeons, the American Surgical Association, and the American College of Surgeons; he had also been chairman of the American Board of Surgery. Thus, UCSF became one of the premier surgical programs in the country. To my delight, Dunphy was, as predicted, an excellent chair. As Goldman, his predecessor, had done before, Dunphy encouraged me to continue with my research and with the development of the UCSF transplant program.

In my free time, I continued looking for help in developing our clinical transplant program. Gotch, the nephrologist I first worked closely with, had a very successful private practice in the San Francisco area. He was an excellent person to associate with, since many of his patients with renal disease (either in his private practice or at the San Francisco county hospital) could end up being transplant candidates. However, I needed someone who was a full-time nephrologist at the University of California Hospital. So, I looked at the individuals at UCSF's Cardiovascular Research Institute. I found someone at the institute who looked like he had an interest in clinical nephrology, Dr. Paul Gulyassy. Like many of the individuals at the institute, Gulyassy was primarily interested in research; to him, the thought of getting involved in clinical work, particularly as it related to the care of patients on dialysis, represented a very unintellectual pursuit. His initial reaction made it difficult for me to try to sell my idea to him. Interestingly enough, after a while, I was able to convince him to be the nephrologist on our exciting, newly developing clinical transplant service. As it turned out, he became a phenomenal clinician, as bright a star with patients as he had been with his research investigations. He and I eventually coauthored a well-received landmark paper (10). Once I recruited him in 1964, the key members of our UCSF transplant team were all in place.

Before performing our first kidney transplant at UCSF, I thought it would be wise to observe one in the most active program at that time, Dr. Thomas Starzl's department at the University of Colorado. Starzl was very kind to allow me to come and observe and to enjoy such a rich and rewarding experience. Since I had been out of surgery for 2½ years doing research, it was good to be in his very active University of Colorado Hospital operating room. I also made rounds on the wards with the clinical transplant staff. The problems they were having with the use of antilymphocyte serum rapidly became apparent to me. This serum was obtained from horses or rabbits that had been injected with lymphocytes removed either from the human thymus (a) during cardiac operations or from lymph nodes in the bodies of recently deceased humans. The resulting unpurified serum could only be given intramuscularly to human transplant patients: the process was extremely painful.

Since lymphocytes are the primary cells that destroy a foreign organ graft, 2 solutions to that problem were to remove lymphocytes through a thoracic duct (b) fistula (c) or to destroy lymphocytes by exposing them, as at Starzl's program, to an antibody directed at their destruction. Antilymphocyte serum had been known since the 19th century to be an effective way of destroying lymphocytes. I came away from Denver feeling confident that we at UCSF could proceed surgically with our first clinical kidney transplant. But I also resolved that we should try to develop an antilymphocyte serum that could be purified to an extent that it could be given intravenously. I wanted so strongly to avoid having to give at UCSF the painful intramuscular injections of antilymphocyte serum that I had observed in the transplant recipients in Colorado, who claimed to do everything in their power to avoid further excruciating injections of what was, in reality, a "toxic" serum.

On returning to San Francisco after my trip to Denver, I found that a veterinarian named Dr. Robert Perper had made an

---

(a) thymus—a lymphoid gland in the upper anterior chest or at the base of the neck
(b) thoracic duct—the main trunk of a system of lymphatic vessels that open into the left subclavian vein under the collarbone
(c) fistula—a surgically created passage

appointment to see me about the possibility of earning a Ph.D. in immunology. Very few people come along like this in a lifetime. With a degree in veterinary medicine, he had built up a veterinary clinic practice that was so successful that he had built several other veterinary clinics elsewhere in northern California. In essence a "McVet" owner, he was making more money than he could spend. He built a magnificent house on top of the highest hill in Sausalito, but clearly was still searching for nonmonetary fulfillment (I remember the house very well, since Mignette and I were once invited there to dinner). It was so high up that Perper couldn't obtain fire insurance, because it was impossible for a fire truck to get up the winding road. From the house the view of the Bay and San Francisco was absolutely glorious.

But on that day in 1963 when Perper and I first met, he said to me that he didn't need to make any more money: what he wanted was a Ph.D. He had the intellectual hunger to pursue another rigorous graduate degree and to try to make a difference in my kidney transplant service; moreover, he didn't need or want a salary from UCSF.

It just so happened, just a few months before Perper first came to my office, that Dr. Keith Reemtsma at Tulane University in New Orleans had reported a kidney heterotransplant (i.e., a transplant between differing species) in a 23-year-old schoolteacher in January 1964. The teacher's new kidney came from a chimpanzee and functioned for 9 months before she died of unrelated causes. A subsequent transplant in Tulane in another human recipient used a kidney from a rhesus monkey, but that graft was rapidly rejected. Also in 1964, Dr. Claude Hitchcock, at what is now Hennepin County Medical Center in Minneapolis, had transplanted a baboon kidney into a 65-year-old woman, but that kidney only lasted 4 days. Starzl in Denver then transplanted baboon kidneys into 6 patients; despite high doses of Imuran (azathioprine) and prednisone—2 powerful immunosuppressive drugs—all 6 of those grafts were also rejected.

I felt that Perper would be an ideal candidate to investigate experimental heterotransplants with me at UCSF, given his veterinary background along with at least the single heterotransplant success achieved by Reemtsma in New Orleans. I also proposed to Perper a second research project involving development of a purified antilymphocyte serum that could be given to patients intravenously. Therefore, at that point, 2 research projects were ongoing in my laboratory. First, we were studying the heterograft response. Second, we were making and testing purified antilymphocyte globulin (ALG), using horses, that could be given intravenously to human patients. So, within a year of my return to San Francisco as a faculty member, 2 major research projects were up and running. We were preparing to perform our first clinical kidney transplant. The organ transplant program at UCSF was well on its way to success.

Chapter Eight
ORGAN TRANSPLANT
PROGRAM AT UCSF

We had now completed all the organizational work with respect to the participants in the kidney transplant team at the University of California, San Francisco (UCSF). We knew what to expect preoperatively and postoperatively in transplant recipients. So, we set a date for our first operation: March 5, 1964. Because of the wide interest in the beginning of this program, we performed the recipient portion of that first transplant at UCSF in one of our operating rooms with a large observational theater above. While we were preparing the anatomic site in the recipient for the kidney graft, the donor team in the next operating room was preparing to remove the kidney. It was being donated by a mother to her 24-year-old daughter. It was a thrill for me to bring the kidney from the donor room into the recipient room.

After perfusion with cold salt solution, the kidney appeared pale. Within 21 minutes after its removal from the mother, we reconstructed its blood supply to the daughter's iliac artery and vein. Once the kidney was successfully transplanted, it immediately became firm and turgid and returned to its normal reddish purple color. The sight of this revascularized kidney was exhilarating for me, as it was for the audience in the observational theater. As urine began to flow from the ureter, the miracle of this organ transplant filled me with awe. Every transplant that I perform still fills me with awe, even now, 45 years later.

By the end of 1964, we had completed a total of 11 kidney transplants using living related donors and 4 kidney transplants using deceased donors. We continued to fine-tune the recipients' immunosuppressive drugs (Imuran and prednisone) in order to achieve the best kidney graft survival rate possible. In addition, we developed techniques for improving donor kidneys, so that better immediate function in the recipient could be achieved (11). The success of our UCSF kidney transplant program was heralded in scientific publications as well as in the local press. Since ours was the only active transplant program in northern California, the list of potential recipients from practicing nephrologists began to grow.

That same year, 1964, Bert Dunphy had come from Oregon to assume the chair of surgery at UCSF. While in Oregon, his last chief resident had been Folkert Belzer, who was sent by Dunphy to England for 1 year to train at Guy's Hospital in London before arriving at UCSF in 1965. As head of the research laboratory, I was asked by Dunphy whether I could find a research project for Belzer, whose primary interest was vascular surgery rather than transplantation. After I talked with Belzer, it became apparent that he had no specific training in immunology, so I looked for a project that would suit his background and current clinical expertise.

As it turned out, I quickly identified a key problem for him to work on. In those early days, when we received an offer of a kidney from a deceased donor, it usually came from one of the many emergency rooms in San Francisco, especially from the San Francisco County Hospital. Once the potential donor was determined to be brain-dead, most often after cardiac arrest, he or she would be placed on a life support system until the kidneys could be removed. Since we had no method of kidney preservation at that time, either of 2 scenarios would ensue. Sometimes, the donor's kidneys would be removed and then rapidly brought to UCSF for transplantation.

At other times, the donor was transported by ambulance from the emergency room to UCSF, then placed in an operating room next to the potential recipient; the kidney transplant would then proceed very much as if using a living donor. This procedure of moving the deceased donor was very awkward for us as well as stressful for the family members.

Therefore, I felt that one of our most pressing needs was to develop a preservation method so that the donor kidney could be removed at a distant site, then preserved and transported to the site of the recipient operation. I explained to Belzer that this would be a good project for him.

By the time Belzer came to UCSF in late 1965, we had performed over 40 kidney transplants. The majority used living related donors, since transporting deceased donors and/or their kidneys was so problematic. Belzer set to work. He initially was able to show that whole-blood perfusion of kidneys in dogs was only possible for a short period, given a rapid rise in perfusion pressure. Thus, he switched his attention to the use of plasma as a perfusing agent, but plasma also eventually resulted in increased perfusion pressure after a slightly longer period. One day, the plasma that he had collected for the next experimental perfusion was not immediately used, because he was reminded by his wife about concert tickets for that evening. So the plasma was frozen overnight. When it was removed from the freezer the next day, and thawed rapidly by hot water, the plasma had become quite turbid—much to Belzer's surprise. Therefore, in order to obtain a clear solution, he filtered the plasma. The turbid material turned out to be lipoproteins, which were removed by the filtration. The filtered plasma worked well, without any increase in perfusion pressure. By adding a membrane oxygenator into the perfusion circuit and using a pulsatile pump, Belzer was able to preserve kidneys for up to 72 hours. This huge advance in our kidney preservation ability enabled us to initiate a more active deceased donor kidney transplant program at UCSF. The new plasma was named by Belzer cryoprecipitated plasma (CPP) (12).

This important discovery by Belzer was truly an example of research serendipity (finding valuable things not sought for). To this day, his method of cold perfusion preservation of kidneys is still used by many transplant programs, though with newer, smaller, and portable units.

Two years after Belzer's first publication in 1967 on perfusion preservation, Geoffrey Collins of the University of California, Los Angeles (UCLA), reported successful preservation of dog kidneys for 30 hours by simple cold storage with a solution containing high concentrations of potassium and glucose (13). The simplicity of this method resulted in its adoption by many centers throughout the world. It is the most common method used today for storage and transportation of organs for transplantation. The only drawback, in the beginning, was its initially short preservation time of, ideally, 24 hours or less, but that time has been extended to 36 hours nowadays.

Back in the mid-1960s at UCSF, we already—thanks to Belzer's research—had the ability to preserve our deceased donor kidneys. We also had developed a method to improve the function of our donor kidneys by diuresing (increasing excretion of urine) deceased donors as well as living donors pretransplant. The next step needed to continue to develop a first-class kidney transplant program was to see whether or not the early reports we had heard of tissue typing, as described by Jean Dausset, would be useful in selecting donors. Dausset first published in 1958 a description of leukocyte antibodies in the sera of blood-transfused patients (for which he was eventually awarded the Nobel Prize in 1980). In his initial report, he described a technique in which white blood cells agglutinated when subjected to this antibody.

In 1957, Dr. Rose Payne of Stanford University reported that antibodies to white cells also occurred in pregnant women. We were very fortunate that Payne (one of the pioneers in tissue typing) was on the faculty at nearby Stanford, which did not have a transplant program; therefore, we could collaborate with her in exploring the role of the human leukocyte antigen (HLA) in transplantation. We could now determine what the possible success of an individual donor-recipient transplant would be, based on the pair's tissue compatibility as determined by Payne's laboratory tests (14) and by Dr. Paul Terasaki, the developer of the Microtest tray at UCLA. This plastic tray has 60 individual 0.001-milliliter wells, allowing for the least amount of typing reagent possible for multiple use.

To achieve the best possible results in kidney transplantation, we also focused on how to improve the immunosuppressive drugs we were using. Although Imuran and prednisone were quite effective, we were disappointed in the 1-year graft and patient survival statistics, both in the group of recipients with living related donors and particularly in the group with deceased donor kidneys. Short of finding another immunosuppressive chemical agent, we explored other techniques of destroying the cells responsible for rejection, namely the peripheral blood lymphocytes. One way that had been proposed by several clinical transplant groups was to create a thoracic duct fistula in which large numbers of lymphocytes could be removed from an individual. Frequently, this technique resulted in early fistula failure for a variety of reasons, including clotting of the fistula and protein depletion of the patient. We examined the possibility of making a more effective thoracic duct fistula; we did the experimental work in goats and were quite successful (15). However, even though 8 million lymphocytes per milliliter could be removed, the effect on suppressing the immune response was still quite limited.

The next possible immunosuppressive technique was to destroy the lymphocytes themselves with serum obtained from either horses or rabbits, directed at the lymphocytes. This technique was only marginally successful in the hands of the group in Colorado—primarily, I felt, because of the severe pain caused from the intramuscular or subcutaneous injection of the antilymphocyte globulin (ALG) they had produced there. The need was urgent to develop a far less painful technique for administration of ALG.

One of the research proposals being investigated by veterinarian Bob Perper involved a purified horse serum directed at human lymphocytes that could be given intravenously. After 2 years of study, he developed a method in which the antibodies to red blood cells could be absorbed and the active material could be purified by using a series of previously published techniques. Thus, our group at UCSF described a rapid and simple method of obtaining large amounts of antibody to lymphocytes from horses (16). We used this technique effectively in goats, reducing the total lymphocyte count by 2- to 3-fold. After 5 weeks of daily intravenous injections of our ALG in goats, we saw no toxic reactions. We now had a preparation that could be duplicated for use against human lymphocytes and given intravenously to patients undergoing a transplant. Our next goal was to find a reliable source of human leukocyte antigens that would result in consistent depression of the immune response.

Perper worked out better than I ever would have anticipated. As my first Ph.D., similar to one's first child, he will always be remembered as special. While completing his project concerning the development of antilymphocyte serum, he also accomplished a series of other studies in transplantation. In one important 1966 article (17), he described experimental kidney heterotransplants in widely divergent species (dogs and pigs). In another pivotal 1966 article, he described experimental kidney heterotransplants in closely related species (goats and sheep) (18). The next year, he reported that immunity after experimental kidney heterotransplants could be transferred by sensitized serum alone (19). These 3 papers turned out to be the foundation of our understanding of experimental heterotransplants: they are still read and referred to today by investigators studying this unique immune response. Perper's work confirmed what Keith Reemtsma reported in 1964 (20) on successful kidney transplants from chimpanzees into humans, namely, that the immune response in transplants between closely related species is not unlike the response in human-to-human transplants. When the species are more divergent, as with the use of baboons or rhesus monkeys as donors for humans, then the reaction is much more severe and, as shown in our UCSF studies, primarily due to antibodies.

Today we cannot use nonhuman primates, for a variety of reasons, as a source of organs for human transplants. So, at the University of Minnesota, we are exploring the use of organs obtained from pigs. Currently, we have been successful in transplanting pancreatic islet cells (which make insulin) from pigs into monkeys (21). Soon we will be embarking on a trial in which human patients will receive pancreatic insulin-producing islet cells from pigs.

All of the building blocks for successful transplants were being developed in the 1960s in the UCSF program. The results of those successes in transplantation would lead to many exciting professional rewards.

Chapter Nine
REWARDS OF SUCCESS

The clinical transplant program at the University of California, San Francisco (UCSF), was progressing extremely well. We were rapidly becoming recognized as one of the pioneer transplant programs in the United States; we were giving presentations not only at local and national but also at international surgical meetings.

One professional reward for this progress came when I was selected by the dean of our medical school to represent UCSF in the competition to be a Markle Scholar in Academic Medicine. Even being nominated to be a Markle Scholar was a singular honor. Only 1 nominee was chosen each year from each of the 90 medical schools in the United States and Canada. This individual had to be destined for a career in academic medicine. To encourage that pursuit, the Markle Scholar program had been established in 1946 by John Russell, formerly of the Carnegie Corporation in New York; the program lasted 22 years (from 1947 to 1969). The 90 nominees each year would meet at several locations throughout the United States, usually in groups of about 12, with the selection committee; only 25 nominees could be chosen each year to be Markle Scholars.

Russell himself had devised a broad-based, in-depth selection process. For the selection committee, he invited presidents and chief executive officers (CEOs) of businesses, university presidents (from almost every university in Canada and the United States), lawyers, clergy, and editors of most of the major newspapers. These luminaries and their spouses would meet for 3 days at a resort site, where each of the 12 nominees would have their breakfast, lunch, and dinner with a committee member and spouse on a rotating basis. Through these informal meals, the selection committee would have an opportunity to get to know the Markle Scholar nominee under normal social circumstances.

After these meals, the nominees and the selection committee members and spouses would discuss literature, including recent books any of us had read, as well as social, ecologic, and economic issues—almost everything imaginable except medicine. These discussions would typically involve 2 nominees at a time, but occasionally all 12 nominees were encouraged to carry on a debate among themselves. The selection committee members and spouses did everything in their power to make the 3 days as pleasant as possible. To that end, they sporadically gave us time off for sports or relaxation. However, I must admit those were 3 of the most emotionally draining days I had spent in a long time. You never knew, at any time, which subjects would be presented for you to discuss.

My particular 3-day session was held at the Broadmoor Hotel in Colorado Springs, a very pleasant site for such an ongoing examination. We each roomed with another nominee, so we had an opportunity to get to know someone from another medical school and we would discuss our impressions of that day's activities. My roommate was Donald Lindberg, a pathologist from the University of Missouri. He currently is the director of the United States National Library of Medicine, a position he has held since 1984. On the last night we were there, he and I tried to make a list of who we thought would become a Markle Scholar and who we thought would not. Interestingly enough, we came pretty close to being correct in most instances.

At the conclusion of the 3 days, I left for a meeting of the Society of University Surgeons in Los Angeles, not knowing how I had fared. After landing in Los Angeles I received a phone call from home about a telegram that had arrived: I had been chosen a Markle Scholar in Academic Medicine. That day was almost as memorable as the day I received notice that I had been accepted into medical school. My $30,000 Markle Scholar award could be used over a 5-year period to supplement research or academic needs. I was now a member of an elite group of academic physicians and surgeons. Interestingly, an analysis of the chosen versus rejected nominees at the end of the program in 1969 showed that among nominees who went on to succeed in academic medicine, almost as many had been rejected as Markle Scholars as had been chosen (22). Obviously, the *nomination* process by the medical schools had been very well done. Again, only 25 of the 90 nominees could be selected each year; in the 22 years of the program, a total of 506 Markle Scholars were chosen.

Those of us chosen for the Markle Scholarship participated in a meeting each year at a resort site somewhere in the United States or Canada, where we presented papers and listened to outstanding invited speakers. These meetings were attended only by the active scholars and our spouses. The various topics encompassed science and the humanities, academic medicine and public policy, medicine in a changing society, motivation in medicine, and other cross-disciplinary themes. These meetings helped us get to know many individuals in the field of academic medicine that we otherwise would never have even met.

In 1969, when John Russell retired, Lloyd Morrisett, also formerly from the Carnegie Corporation, became the new director of the Markle Foundation. Unfortunately, Morrisett felt that the Markle Scholar program had run its course and announced that the foundation would embark on an ambitious program in the field of mass communication. By the time the amazing Markle Scholar program ended, an average of $2 million had been disbursed annually, building on the $15 million originally endowed by businessman John Markle.

As a Markle Scholar in Academic Medicine, I was able to enjoy even more fully my well-balanced life as a surgeon-scientist. Our rapidly growing, quite successful clinical program in renal transplantation at UCSF was complemented by our ongoing research programs. Surgery department chairman Bert Dunphy was growing concerned as to whether I would stay at UCSF. Early in 1966, he convinced Clark Kerr, the 12th president of the entire University of California system, that I should be promoted, in order to ensure my retention. Thus, President Kerr promoted me from a third-step assistant professor to a second-step full professor of surgery, an unprecedented leap. Years later, when I received the

Glenn T. Seaborg Award in 1996, I had a chance to meet Clark Kerr once again: he confirmed that he had not supported such a promotion for anyone else in the University of California system in all the years (1958-1967) that he was president. In addition, also in 1966, Dunphy appointed me vice chairman of the UCSF surgery department. With this dual promotion, I felt I would most likely stay at UCSF. Dunphy stated that, when he retired, I would be the logical person to become the new chairman of the surgery department at UCSF.

I continued to be recruited for surgery department chairman positions by various medical schools and surgery departments throughout the United States. I was marketable as a very attractive candidate, given my status as a pioneer in the newly developing, exciting field of transplantation, particularly with my years in basic science research. Several visits I made as a chairman candidate were quite interesting. I'm often reminded in particular of my visit to the University of North Carolina in Chapel Hill. The dean of the medical school was Ike Taylor, a Harvard graduate and a very conservative Ivy League internist. On the evening that he invited me to his house for dinner, I had the opportunity to meet his son, who was sitting on the floor in their living room playing the guitar and looking just like the long-haired hippies that I had known in San Francisco. Ike Taylor told me at the time that he was concerned that his son would not amount to much. However, JAMES Taylor went on to become a very popular and successful folk singer. Unfortunately, the University of North Carolina lacked adequate research facilities for surgery. At that time, they were using semitrucks backed up to a platform as research laboratories until they could build proper facilities. I therefore was not persuaded to go there.

I was subsequently invited to New York University (NYU) Medical Center, which uses Bellevue Hospital as their medical facility. This chairman position was very tempting. Some of the most outstanding immunologists in the country were working at NYU at the time. However, as persuasive as my colleagues in immunology were, I couldn't see raising 4 sons on the east side of Manhattan. If we moved to what we considered a reasonable suburban area, I would have had to spend at least 2 hours driving to and from work every day. I felt, with my young career and family, that such a long commute would represent an inappropriate loss of time and not be in anyone's best interest.

I received a call 3 or 4 months later from Cornell University in New York City to come there as the chief of surgery. I told them that I wasn't interested, because I had already considered NYU and felt that it would be difficult for me to raise my kids in New York City. I certainly didn't want to spend excessive time traveling back and forth to work. The vice president of health affairs and the dean of Cornell were very upset, stating this was the prestigious CORNELL, not NYU: how could I turn them down over the phone? They asked if I would mind if they came out to San Francisco to discuss this matter directly. I told them that it probably wouldn't change my mind, but that they were certainly welcome to come. They did come for a visit. They saw my office overlooking the Golden Gate Bridge and the Pacific Ocean and realized the convenience of my adjacent laboratories. They then came to our Twin Peaks home, which the money obtained from my promotion had enabled us to buy. From almost every room, our house afforded a breathtaking view of both the San Francisco Bay Bridge and the Golden Gate Bridge, as well as all of downtown San Francisco. The Cornell contingent went back east with an appreciation of why I did not want to leave San Francisco or forsake the situation I had at UCSF.

Of the 11 medical schools that tried to recruit me to be chairman of their surgery department, only a few were actually tempting, albeit fleetingly. I felt that I would probably stay at UCSF and eventually become chairman once Dunphy retired.

I had reached many of my professional goals, including a successful and rapidly growing clinical transplant program and a productive research effort. We were presenting our clinical and research papers at transplant and surgical meetings throughout the country and abroad. I had competed for, and eventually received, a very large program project grant from the National Institutes of Health (NIH) to support our clinical transplant activity (currently in its 40ᵗʰ year). In addition, my first Ph.D. student, Bob Perper, successfully defended his thesis and obtained his Ph.D. in transplantation surgery at UCSF. On the personal side, we relished our spectacular home on Twin Peaks. Even though we did not know many of our neighbors on a first-name basis, our neighborhood included many intriguing San Franciscans, among them Mr. Melvin Belli, the celebrated trial attorney, who lived just down the street from us on Glenbrook Avenue. Except for the bad summer weather in San Francisco, which is always foggy and cold, it appeared as though we had everything we would ever want.

Yet on closer look, there were some major distractions in our personal life. The drug culture in San Francisco was growing rapidly. The infamous Haight-Ashbury area was just below our medical center and extended into Golden Gate Park. In the mid-1960s, San Francisco became the hippie capital of the United States. Many youngsters began coming to San Francisco, initially as flower children and eventually as pot-smoking hippies. By 1967 (on the heels of the famed "Summer of Love"), harder drugs were introduced, such as LSD and eventually cocaine. The number of hippies in the Haight-Ashbury and Golden Gate Park area increased to a point where it was difficult for my wife to take our children to enjoy the recreational activities available. It was not unusual for her to relate to me a story of hippies walking through the park carrying crosses, bombed out of their minds on drugs, some clothed and some unclothed. There seemed to be very little official police control of such activities. This state of affairs represented a threat to the safety of Mig and the boys and was certainly a bad example for my sons in their formative years. Sadly, my beloved San Francisco had become the Sodom and Gomorrah of the west!

In addition, it became apparent that Dunphy would continue as department chairman for some time to come. As the years progressed, I would lose some of the cachet that I had earned with my academic accomplishments in transplantation and research. It also concerned me that the longer I stayed there, the less likely I would be considered as a replacement for Dunphy, since deans frequently look for new blood.

Thus, I began to have a new interest in becoming a surgery department chairman so that I could implement my own training program. I wanted to develop academic surgeons with a specific expertise not only in clinical surgery but also in basic and applied research. This was not happening at UCSF, where most of the staff were more concerned with their clinical practices and were really only mentors for clinical training. Most of the faculty were excellent clinical surgeons, having been trained by standout department chairmen H. Glenn Bell and then Leon Goldman, but were not expressly dedicated to education or research. Thus, I had not closed my mind to the possibility of an appropriate offer, if it came from a medical school in a community that would provide an excellent place to raise our 4 boys and that would give me an opportunity to put into practice my thoughts on training academic surgeons, in general as well as transplant surgery.

Such an opportunity did come to pass in December 1966, when I was visited by 2 gentlemen that I very much admired. The first was Dr. Richard Varco, who was a master surgeon and one of the major strengths of the surgery department at the University of Minnesota in Minneapolis. His role in helping develop the groundbreaking cardiac surgical program at Minnesota was well known throughout the United States. In addition, he had performed the first kidney transplant at Minnesota in 1963 between identical-twin sisters. The second visitor from Minnesota was Dr. Robert Good, one of the foremost immunologists in the country, who had performed the world's first bone marrow transplant in 1968. Varco and Good (who had also been a Markle Scholar) arrived at my doorstep in an effort to persuade me to look at the possibility of becoming chairman of the surgery department at the University of Minnesota, a position held by Dr. Owen Wangensteen for 37 years. Wangensteen had built an exemplary surgery department that had trained countless academic surgeons and surgery department chairs.

After discussing their compelling proposal with Mignette, who was a native Minnesotan, I decided to accept their invitation to look at Minnesota. My visit to Minnesota would have to occur sometime in January 1967, after the Christmas holidays. Being a native Californian, I felt some trepidation at the prospect of visiting Minnesota in January. But going there under the worst weather circumstances also seemed to be a good way to see if this would be an advisable move for me. As an aside, even though Mignette was totally supportive, I recognized that she had purposely left the cold climate of Minnesota to come to California to launch an adventurous career as a nurse. Having married a Californian, she assumed she would most likely be staying in the state of California. However, she never once expressed any opposition to my looking at the position being vacated by Wangensteen and to our possibly moving back to Minnesota. Of course, the Minnesota that she remembered was on a 160-acre farm near Benson, a small town in the western part of the state. Growing up in the 1930s and 1940s, she had only outdoor plumbing and no real control of the weather, either the heat or the cold. Certainly, if I accepted the position there, we would have a home in Minneapolis, far different from the farmhouse of her youth.

Therefore, despite my accelerated promotion by President Clark Kerr, my position as vice chairman of the surgery department at UCSF, and all of the accolades that I had received in San Francisco, I now was off to seriously consider moving to another medical center.

Chapter Ten
WHY MINNESOTA?

After I turned down 11 offers from university medical school programs to direct their surgery department, and after I received an accelerated promotion and appointment to vice chairman of the surgery department at the University of California, San Francisco (UCSF), many of my friends and colleagues found out that I was planning to look at Minnesota. They asked, why Minnesota?

The person who most vociferously asked that question was my own mother. In the United States, she had only lived on the East or West Coast: first in Boston and primarily in California (in San Francisco and then Oakland). She pointed out to me that there was very little but farmland in the middle of the United States, in particular in the northern part of the Midwest, where the temperature would be "very cold" in the winter. She used an Armenian phrase that meant "I must be crazy" [meaning me!] to go to Minnesota to look at a possible position.

To my mother and to others, I explained that both Bob Good and Dick Varco, my visitors from the University of Minnesoa Medical School faculty, were extremely persuasive. They already were good friends of mine. I would go back at the most extreme time of winter, namely in January, so that I could see for myself if Minneapolis would be an acceptable place to live. When I flew to Minnesota and rented a car, the temperature there was below zero (I believe 5 or 10 degrees below). With a proper overcoat, I found that this temperature was not a major problem. While I was in the rental car, I listened to the radio and learned that the wind chill (a term I had never heard before) was something like 25 degrees below zero. I thought the radio announcer was saying that the temperature on the windshield of the car would be 25 degrees below zero. I soon found out what wind chill meant, but once again I was able to tolerate it.

When I arrived at the medical school on the main Minneapolis campus, I found a very pleasant and amiable dean in Dr. Robert Howard. He arranged for meetings with each member of the surgery department faculty as well as with each of the other department chairs.

Early on, I was impressed that the medical school's other department chairs were extremely receptive to the possibility of my coming to Minnesota. This was nice to hear. In particular, I found it easy to talk with the chairs of the major medical school departments, such as medicine, pediatrics, and pathology. Since I would be spending time with them at various medical school functions, it was gratifying to see that they would be a genial and cooperative group. As far as the surgery department was concerned, the faculty members were all quite pleasant. However, there definitely was a split, in that part of the department felt that a local candidate should become the chair. The local candidate who was most interested in the position was Dr. C. Walton Lillehei, the world-renowned chief of cardiac surgery. A small group of advocates for choosing Dr. Lillehei as the next chair included his brother, Dr. Richard C. Lillehei, also a distinguished professor and surgeon. Still, I did not sense any strong feeling from the rest of the department regarding that possibility.

I had a gracious meeting with Dr. Owen Wangensteen, the chair of surgery since 1930, although it was evident that he, too, favored his former resident Walt Lillehei to succeed him.

The other surgery department faculty members all shared helpful information with me and were open to my assuming the helm. One intriguing aspect of Minnesota's surgery department was that every faculty member had a research grant and a research laboratory. Some of the laboratories were small; others used a large common laboratory in the basement of the medical school building. It soon became evident why they all had research grants. When they were appointed by Wangensteen, they were each told that any secretary's salary would only be paid for by a research grant and that any travel would only be possible if they had a research grant. As a result, they all applied; eventually, those who stayed were successful in obtaining a research grant, either from the National Institutes of Health (NIH) or from local granting agencies. Such wide grant support to cover faculty travel as well as secretarial and other academic support was unique. I had not seen anything like it at the other 11 medical schools I had considered moving to. I felt strongly that the foundation of academic medicine was research. The University of Minnesota had clearly been comprehensively organized in that direction by Wangensteen.

In the mid-1960s, only 2 major institutions in the United States trained academic surgeons. One was Johns Hopkins Hospital in Baltimore, a program developed by Dr. William Stewart Halsted, considered by many the father of American surgery. Halsted was also the founder of the distinctly American-style surgical residency training program, a format that entailed progressive clinical responsibility. The program he developed at Johns Hopkins was the first residency program in the United States. It consisted of an internship of variable length, followed by 6 years as an assistant resident (rotating on various general surgical and surgical speciality areas) and 2 years as a house surgeon: 8 or more years total, with a primary emphasis on clinical surgery.

The other institution that trained most of the academic surgeons in the United States was Minnesota, under Wangensteen's direction. His philosophy was strongly weighted toward research, with minimal emphasis on clinical surgery. The strong research base in Minnesota became my paramount reason for seriously considering the position as surgery department chair. I feel that it is possible to clinically train research surgeons, but that it is almost impossible for clinically trained surgeons to become research investigators. This philosophy definitely became my primary motivation for coming to Minnesota.

In addition, that January of 1967, there was a buzz around Minnesota's surgery department regarding 2 transplants that had been carried out there in diabetic patients the month before. The first was a segmental pancreas transplant on December 17, 1966, performed by Dr. William Kelly using a duct-ligated segmental (partial) pancreas graft plus a kidney graft. Unfortunately, the pancreas graft developed a fistula (an opening to the outside); the recipient was free of insulin for only 6 days and eventually required removal of both the kidney graft and the pancreas graft. The second pancreas transplant, in a 32-year-old recipient, was performed on New Year's Eve by Richard Lillehei; this operation included the entire pancreas and the duodenum (the first part of the small intestine), which was brought out as a fistula. Thus, in this department that so solidly encouraged amply funded research, 2 world-first transplants had just been performed: the first-ever pancreas transplant and the first-ever intestinal transplant. I felt that Minnesota could provide an ideal environment for continuing to develop a world-class transplant unit. (Its first kidney transplant had been performed nearly 4 years earlier, on June 7, 1963.)

Minnesota's research laboratory space was quite adequate, so when I accepted the position, I really only made 2 initial requests to the dean, much to his surprise. The first was a request for 2 Gopher football tickets on the 50-yard line. The second was a request to be able to fly first-class (because of my size). Thus, I could actually do work while on the plane, since as the new department chairman, I would need to travel extensively to recruit faculty and residents and to obtain research grants. Minneapolis's central location would make it easy for me to fly to the East Coast or to the West Coast or down South, cutting some of the total travel time necessary in the career of a young academic surgeon.

During that January 1967 visit to Minneapolis, I had an opportunity to talk with surgeons and physicians I knew who now lived in Minneapolis. I found out that it was an ideal setting to raise children, since Minneapolis seemed very much like the United States of 20 years earlier. The "City of Lakes," as it is still nicknamed, was not caught up in the drug culture and other antisocial problems that had developed in other cities, such as San Francisco, at that time. So, I called my wife to tell her that I had accepted the position and we would be moving to Minnesota. I'm sure that she was shocked, but she seemed to look forward to the move. In a way, it was coming home for her, particularly with the relatives that she still had in

Benson, Minnesota, and 2 sisters who lived in the Twin Cities (Minneapolis and its next-door neighbor, St. Paul, the state capital).

Three weeks later, in February 1967, I went to a Society of University Surgeons meeting in Toronto. On returning from that meeting, I stopped in Minneapolis, where I had been scheduled to meet with a realtor to look at houses. A wonderful real estate agent from a local company showed me all the possible areas to live. We rapidly excluded the Minnetonka area, which was west of town—as it would mean a long drive coming in against the sunlight in the morning and going against the sunlight at night. I felt it was simply too far away from the medical center. We therefore looked within the city of Minneapolis. In our travels, the realtor and I came at last to Lake Harriet, which is a perfect lake, spring fed and surrounded by big beautiful homes. I said to the realtor that if one of those homes on the east side of the lake ever became available I certainly would be quite interested. I flew back home and arrived early on a Sunday, since I was scheduled in the operating room at UCSF on Monday.

That Sunday morning, I received a phone call from the realtor, who reported that one of those houses on the east side of Lake Harriet was going to come up for sale. The wealthy family who owned it had initially thought of giving it as a parsonage for their church, but had now decided to sell it and had asked the local bank to give them a potential asking price. The realtor told me that 12 people had already been lined up for that Monday morning to tour the house. If Mignette and I were interested, we would have to make a down payment right then and there, in order to buy the house before it was seen by the 12.

It's difficult to buy a house that you have not seen. Therefore, Mignette called her sister, Violet Mae (who lived in Mendota Heights, a suburb southeast of Minneapolis), and asked her if she would go and look at the home and describe it to us. Violet Mae, a precise person, went to the house and spent 2 hours inspecting it. She phoned us and, in a 2-hour call, described in detail each room of the house. I then rapidly called the realtor back and told him that we would buy it and I would send him a check.

Unbelievably, this 10,000-square-foot English Tudor house—with 7 bedrooms, 9 bathrooms, a large library, and an entertainment room located on 3 city lots overlooking one of the most beautiful lakes in Minneapolis—was being sold for significantly less than $100,000. The primary reason for the low price was that many people in this upper-middle-class area of Minneapolis had moved out to Lake Minnetonka, now that the freeway to the west of town had been completed. Once again, the question "why Minnesota?" was answered with a wonderful place to live and a wonderful place to work, both in Minneapolis. No longer was the question "why Minnesota?" Instead, it was "why not Minnesota?" and I could find no reason why not. And, 42 years later, Mignette and I still live in that same wonderful house and I still work in that same wonderful surgery department.

Chapter Eleven
MINNESOTA BEGINNINGS

The trip from San Francisco to Minneapolis in June 1967 was quite uneventful, as compared with some of our other trips. We of course were all sad to leave, the boys because they were leaving their very good friends and schoolmates, and Mignette and I because we were leaving the beautiful Bay area, in particular, our lovely house on Twin Peaks. In the back of my mind, I could hear Tony Bennett singing "I left my heart in San Francisco—high on a hill, it calls to me." Professionally, I was sad to leave. As vice chairman of the University of California, San Francisco (UCSF), surgery department, I had all the advantages of being a professor and vice chairman, yet I didn't have to attend the many committee meetings or attend to the umpteen administrative tasks that were all handled so ably by the chairman, Dr. J. Englebert Dunphy. However, my family and I knew that Minneapolis was our future. We were all very much looking forward to this next, and hopefully last, move of my peripatetic academic journey.

We were very fortunate in that a young man who was working for me in the UCSF research laboratories preceded us to Minneapolis, where he met the movers and took the responsibility for arranging our furniture, rugs, paintings, and other belongings in our new house overlooking Lake Harriet. I can only guess that the young man had some prior experience with interior decorating, since he did such a magnificent job. When we arrived, it was already a well-organized, fully appointed home that we could have shown off to the public if we had been so inclined. Quite frankly, we made very few changes to the furniture's positioning during the course of the next few weeks as we settled in.

As soon as we showed up at the house, our 4 boys took off and went down to explore Lake Harriet. Each of the 4 corners of the lake at that time featured a lifeguard. The boys were so excited by this beautiful, swimmable lake right there in front of our house that we did not see them until suppertime. We will never forget their comment that first evening: "Thank you, Mom and Dad, for bringing us to Minneapolis." The lake was ours, and life for them would become very enjoyable from here on.

Another wonderful surprise was the Lyndale Park Rose Garden only half a block from our house. This jewel celebrated its 100th birthday in July 2008 and remains as lovely now as it was when we first strolled through it. The second oldest rose garden in the United States, it showcases 100 varieties of 3,000 plants. It was designed by Theodore Wirth, who was also the mastermind of the nation's oldest public rose garden, in Hartford, Connecticut, which was constructed beginning in 1903 during his park superintendency there. Wirth's son went on to direct the national park system during the Truman, Eisenhower, Kennedy, and Johnson presidencies and, tapping his father's archives, to oversee the development of the White House Rose Garden.

In addition, a bandstand just beyond the rose garden played host to the Minneapolis Pops and various other instrumental groups almost every night from Memorial Day to Labor Day. It was just like being in the center of a small town in the Midwest, with popcorn and ice cream concessions as part of the bandstand. People in their boats and all along the shore would listen to the concert each summer night. We could actually sit on our porch and hear the band, without even having to go down to the lake. I could imagine nothing more ideal than our living situation at that point. Any doubts that any member of the family might have harbored about the move were completely erased.

Once we were settled, I went to the University of Minnesota surgery department and began looking at what I needed to do as a beginning. Dr. William Kelly, the titular head of the transplant group, had resigned. Although Dr. Owen Wangensteen, the department chairman from January 1930 through June 1967, had appointed him head of clinical transplantation, the transplant program had unfortunately been running by committee rather than by his direction. He had to deal with the very strong personalities of

Drs. Richard Varco, Richard Lillehei, and J. Bradley Aust. I'm sure that frustration was primarily responsible for Kelly's resignation. He then went into private practice in Minneapolis and followed his second clinical love, cardiac surgery. He enjoyed a long career as a private practice cardiac surgeon in the Minneapolis area.

Therefore, in early July 1967, I had no one on board to help me with the transplant program's administration. My first endeavor was to find a transplant surgeon to lead that group. Earlier that year, at the international Transplantation Society meeting in Paris, I had been fortunate enough to meet Dr. Richard Simmons. I had been introduced to him by Dr. Anthony Monaco, a colleague from Harvard. Dick Simmons and I had a very productive conversation, at which time I told him I was looking for someone to help me develop a world-class transplant program at the University of Minnesota. He rapidly responded that he would be very anxious to do so. Of all the recruitment decisions that I have ever made, that had to be one of the best. Simmons was and is an outstanding academic surgeon. A graduate of Harvard University, with honors, he had trained at Columbia-Presbyterian Hospital in New York City, then at Massachusetts General Hospital in Boston under Dr. Paul Russell. Simmons served on the surgical staff at Columbia University's College of Physicians and Surgeons from 1965 to 1968, when he came to Minnesota.

In addition to Simmons, I knew that I needed someone in the field of nephrology who could take care of renal failure patients and be responsible for the dialysis service, which, when I arrived, was being run by surgical residents. I had previously met Dr. Carl Magnus Kjellstrand, who had come to the United States in 1958 with an M.D. as well as a Ph.D. from the University of Lund in Sweden. He had also obtained clinical training as a docent in internal medicine at the famed Karolinska Institute in Stockholm. He was now the director of dialysis at Bethesda Lutheran Hospital in St. Paul (the capital of Minnesota and the twin to Minneapolis, just minutes away). All of the reports from St. Paul were that Kjellstrand was an outstanding clinical physician, basically a surgeon masquerading as an internist. He had been trained in Sweden by the outstanding nephrologist Professor Nils Alwall, who while at the University of Lund developed one of the first clinically useful artificial kidneys and was the only one doing dialysis in that country at that time. Kjellstrand certainly was the dialysis expert I was looking for and became the second person I hired. His appointment was as essential as that of Simmons. Kjellstrand, too, turned out to be as good as I could possibly imagine. He was the kind of doctor who would be on duty long after 5:00 at night. If there was an in-house patient who was sick, Kjellstrand would be there, whether it was 1:00, 2:00, or 3:00 in the morning. This unusual trait (especially for an internist), this degree of clinical dedication, made me feel that, if I were ever sick, I would certainly like Kjellstrand as my physician. Thus, with Simmons and Kjellstrand, we were ready to really embark on our Minnesota transplant program.

I encouraged Richard Lillehei to continue with his pursuit of pancreas transplantation, which represented one of the most exciting things going on in our surgery department in the late 1960s. I actually assisted Lillehei on several kidney-pancreas transplants for diabetic patients. After my initial experience with such transplants, I rapidly formed the impression that this operation was, in fact, too much for patients with brittle type 1 insulin-dependent diabetes.* Early posttransplant, the kidney or pancreas graft, or both, would almost inevitably be rejected by the recipient's immune system. Some of the pancreas and kidney grafts did function for up to 3 or 4 months, but all of them, except for 1, eventually failed in the first year posttransplant. That 1 recipient did have normal function of both the pancreas and kidney graft for 1 year, but on the 1-year anniversary of the transplant, for reasons unknown, committed suicide (tragically, a common problem with diabetics).

I thus felt that our clinical transplant program at the University of Minnesota should examine other types of transplants. Unfortunately, diabetic patients in renal failure were not being

---

*Type 1 diabetes (formerly called juvenile) is an autoimmune disease that destroys the pancreas's beta cells, which make insulin. Insulin-dependent patients show no evidence of insulin production in their own body, so must depend on outside insulin. "Brittle" here means labile or uncontrollable diabetes.

offered either a transplant or dialysis. It was a very sad situation, given the 1½ million type 1 diabetic patients in the United States at that time, 50% of whom would eventually die of renal failure. Most dialysis programs in the late 1960s would not accept diabetic patients because they were very difficult to care for, especially with their many diabetic complications. Moreover, transplant surgeons worldwide would not offer even a kidney transplant to diabetic patients; the feeling was that the use of steroids (part of the required immunosuppressive drug regimen posttransplant) would make the insulin management of their diabetes almost impossible.

In 1968, I decided that we should start offering kidney transplants alone (i.e., without a simultaneous pancreas transplant) to diabetic patients. This represented an opportunity for diabetics to be treated for at least 1 of the conditions (renal failure) that could eventually lead to their death, even without a pancreas transplant to treat their lack of insulin production. Our results with transplanting kidneys alone in diabetic patients proved that they could undergo a transplant with the same degree of success as nondiabetic patients. For the first 2 to 3 years posttransplant, their kidney graft survival rates and patient survival rates were equivalent to those of nondiabetic kidney transplant recipients. After 2 to 3 years posttransplant, however, the kidney graft survival rates and patient survival rates for diabetic recipients decreased.

This falloff was primarily due to patient deaths from the dire vascular (blood vessel) complications of diabetes, such as myocardial infarction (heart attack), stroke, or other peripheral vascular disease. If you examined the graft loss rates in a death-censored analysis (i.e., eliminating from the analysis patients who died with a functioning kidney graft and considering only patients who still survived posttransplant), then the kidney graft survival rate for our type 1 diabetic kidney transplant recipients was the same as for our nondiabetic kidney transplant recipients.

All of our main transplant team members were in place: Kjellstrand, Simmons, and me, along with transplant coordinator Justine Willmert, R.N. Willmert had been with me at UCSF. We were ready to launch a new course for clinical transplantation at the

University of Minnesota. However, we lacked an immunosuppressive agent to add to our prevailing posttransplant regimen of Imuran (azathioprine) and prednisone (a steroid), a regimen currently used by all transplant units. As mentioned in the previous chapter, Dr. Robert Perper at UCSF had devised a technique for preparing a suitable antilymphocyte serum that could be given intravenously to patients, without pain, in order to reduce their total lymphocyte numbers. The only problem was that the lymphocytes used to stimulate the horses to form antibody were often inconsistent in both quantity and quality. So, we examined the possibility of instead using lymphocytes grown in tissue culture.

We turned our attention to Roswell Park Cancer Institute (in Buffalo, New York), whose staff members were growing lymphocytes in large numbers. We adapted their technique and began growing large numbers of lymphocytes in culture. We now had consistent lymphocyte numbers and could give any number of lymphocytes to a horse. The end result was a consistent antibody capacity for destroying lymphocytes in our transplant recipients.

Next, we needed to find a place where we could obtain horses for further developing our improved antilymphocyte serum. Very fortunately, we were able to collaborate with the University of Minnesota's veterinary school in nearby St. Paul. We discovered that their faculty had a group of horses used for gynecologic examinations by veterinary students: we could use these horses for our studies. We would be able to pay the veterinary students for injecting and bleeding the horses—the added income was very much appreciated by the students. Our method involved the following steps: First, we injected 5×10^9 lymphocytes in 4 to 9 sites under the skin of the horse. After the third injection, we would then bleed the horses of 9 liters of serum over 7 to 10 days. We then used rabbits to make sure each batch of serum contained no pyrogens (fever-producing substances), before injecting the serum into our transplant recipients, intravenously at about 4 milligrams per kilogram of body weight.

We tested the effectiveness of this serum, to be known as Minnesota antilymphocyte globulin (MALG), by placing full-thickness skin grafts on volunteer patients with multiple sclerosis. They had agreed to this clinical research trial in the hope that MALG would help fight their disease. Skin grafts are the most difficult of all transplanted organs to survive the engraftment process, but the skin grafts of the volunteers who received MALG had an extended survival time: double that of the control group of skin graft recipients who did not receive MALG. We now had a consistent formulation of ALG that had been proven effective in our clinical research trial and could be used for our transplant recipients. The new Minnesota clinical transplant program was well on its way.

Turning my attention to the research laboratory, I felt several major areas had to be investigated. My first priority was our continuing interest in pancreas transplantation. It was now obvious, as described above, that whole-organ pancreas transplants were too big of an operation for brittle diabetic patients; a lesser operation would be preferable. Dr. Arnold Lazarow, the then-chairman of the University of Minnesota's anatomy department, had reported, back in 1960, success in animal experiments with isolating the islets of Langerhans (which contain the beta cells that produce insulin). Using his technique, I was confident that we could isolate islets from animal pancreases and transplant them into diabetic animals, to see if we could cure their diabetes. The islets themselves represent less than 2% of the entire pancreas, so they could be suspended in solution and injected into animals, thus avoiding the larger operation of a whole-organ transplant. If these experiments worked, we could begin isolating human islets to see if transplanting them into diabetic patients would result in a cure. I gave this project initially to Dr. Edward Etheredge, who began working on the isolation and transplantation of islets in laboratory animals.

My second research priority was to continue Perper's heterotransplant experiments, which he had begun at UCSF (where he had decided to stay), to see if it would be possible to successfully transplant organs between animals of differing species. I proposed trying a variety of chemical immunosuppressants, as well as irradiation and plasmapheresis (removal of naturally occurring antibodies), to determine if any of these techniques could result in a successful transplant between animals of differing species. This series of research projects were given to Drs. Martin Mozes and Alan Shons.

My third research priority was to develop a portable perfusion apparatus that would allow for cold storage of kidney grafts while they were transported from deceased donors to waiting recipients. This project would involve downsizing the perfusion apparatus that had been developed by Dr. Folkert Belzer at UCSF. I gave this project to Dr. Allen Moberg.

With these 3 research priorities and a successfully staffed clinical transplant program, I felt that things were progressing well. Now I could turn my attention to effectively structuring the surgical training program for academic surgeons, as well as academic transplant surgeons, at the University of Minnesota.

Chapter Twelve
THE MAKING OF AN
ACADEMIC SURGEON

Now that the University of Minnesota transplant program was in full swing, I began looking at the surgical residency program that had produced so many academic surgeons from the 1930s through mid-1960s. The first thing I noted was that each of the surgical faculty members was expected to pursue a line of research where residents might work with them. Owen Wangensteen (department chair, 1930 to mid-1967) thought that surgical residents should "spend only a limited part of their time in the care of patients and in attendance of operations. They needed to learn to operate, certainly—however, they must also learn to perform such routine duties as the insertion of intravenous tubes and, once mastered, little more was to be learned by endless repetition of such tasks." Wangensteen felt that "surgical residents needed time to read, to think, and to try out their ideas in the laboratories." He would not have them be "mere intellectual parasites using ideas and methods developed by others. They must contribute to the patrimony of their subject"(23).

It was obvious that Wangensteen very passionately believed in looking for the smartest individuals and then obtaining the needed resources and funds. He was able to appoint large numbers of residents: some could do hospital work, while the rest were learning experimental physiology, pursuing research projects in the laboratory, or reading in the library. If the training that a resident needed was not available in our medical school, Wangensteen would send them to another university. Often, residents were sent elsewhere to study physiology; a common destination was the University of Chicago to work with Dr. Maurice Visscher. In 1936, Visscher returned to Minnesota; he and Wangensteen developed a joint physiology-surgery seminar, and many residents spent a full year working in physiology with Visscher.

In addition to his many other accomplishments, Wangensteen introduced the routine of the department weekly review of complications that unfortunately occurred during surgical operations, including a merciless analysis of how and why mistakes were made and how they could be avoided in the future. To the best of my knowledge, Wangensteen's initiative represented the first formal mortality and morbidity conference at any university surgery department. In these sessions, surgical faculty members were unsparing of one another, not with the intent to be cruel, but in order to avoid perpetuation of false ideas or slipshod practices.

Dr. Morley Cohen of Winnipeg, Canada, after a visit to Minnesota in 1952, commented, "I was impressed with the broad yet fundamental approach to the magnitude of surgical problems during these sessions [grand rounds], which were carried on in an atmosphere of competitive informality. The staff said what they thought to be right, no doubt many were wrong, but they certainly were sure nonetheless. Few pussy-footed around the accomplishments or deficiencies of the clinical and research problems that were brought forth at these sessions." Cohen was "impressed by the frequently imaginative suggestions made by Wangensteen during these discussions." After Cohen came to Minnesota as a surgical resident in 1954, he found the training program "often seemingly chaotic, residents disappearing to the research labs for extended periods of time, then returning and sometimes leaving again for another interval. Nevertheless, such constant change and unpredictability stimulated residents to do their utmost to accomplish some research that could establish their identity. A further feature of the surgical program in Minnesota, unusual at the time, was that it was open to anyone with ability, regardless of race, creed, or color. People of diverse races from many countries came to Minnesota for surgical training. This created an active and inquiring atmosphere in the department"(29).

In 1968, as I looked over the Minnesota surgical residency program in general, I found slightly fewer than 100 residents and slightly more than 100 surgical beds. Most of the residents were in a laboratory somewhere. As many as 5 or 6 residents could be on a hospital surgical service that included fewer than 12 inpatients. No question, the clinical opportunities for residents were quite limited and were not a priority under the Wangensteen system. In addition, it was difficult to determine an individual resident's surgical training program, since each program was unique. Some residents spent 1 year on the hospital's surgical service after their internship year and then went directly to a research laboratory, whereas other residents had 1, 2, or possibly 3 clinical years and then went to the research laboratory. It was also difficult to determine how and why individuals eventually came out of the laboratory. When they did, they often ended up as chief residents, even though they may have had only a single clinical year of exposure before their research years.

Amazingly, Wangensteen found funds for all of these surgical residents. He did not charge wealthy patients for surgery, but asked them to contribute to the surgical training program. The department also had 2 or 3 training grants from the National Institutes of Health, along with some local training grants. So, all of the nearly 100 residents were somehow paid a reasonable, but not always adequate, salary. Residents supplemented their salary through moonlighting, primarily at 2 private hospitals in town, namely, North Memorial in the northern suburb of Robbinsdale and Abbott Northwestern near downtown Minneapolis. Although moonlighting was looked down on by the American College of Surgeons, it certainly served a useful purpose in Wangensteen's program: it allowed clinical exposure for residents who were spending time in the research laboratory and needed to keep abreast of clinical surgery. Officially, I did not support moonlighting, but I recognized that it did have worthwhile benefits.

Wangensteen's training program was difficult to analyze, but, obviously, in many ways, it was quite successful. The only downside was that some graduates ended up inadequately trained clinically and never were able to reach the full potential of a well-trained clinical academic surgeon. My former chief of surgery at the University of California, San Francisco (UCSF), Dr. J. Englebert Dunphy, described the program at Minnesota as a "mysterious tunnel in which an individual would enter and eventually leave as a trained academic surgeon. What occurred within the tunnel remained a mystery."

Analyzing Wangensteen's program as it stood, I knew it had many good qualities. However, it needed a more organized approach while maintaining a strong research direction. I felt that, initially, residents should spend 3 years doing clinical surgery, so that they would know whether or not they could be a capable surgeon and whether or not they enjoyed doing surgery. Similarly, the faculty would also know whether or not residents were capable of doing surgery. After those first 3 clinical years, residents would spend 2 to 4 years in the research laboratory, simultaneously working toward either a master's degree or a Ph.D. in physiology, in immunology, in genetics, or in surgery itself. After this research time, residents could then complete their training with 1 year as a senior resident, involving very active surgical exposure, and then a final year as the administrative chief resident on the surgical service.

To accomplish my goals for the refined residency program, I needed to find more clinical exposure than was offered by the slightly more than 100 surgical beds at the University of Minnesota's hospital, most of which were occupied by cardiac surgery patients. The first place I considered was the Minneapolis Veterans Administration (now Affairs) hospital (VA), a few miles south of campus. Dr. Edward Humphrey was the chief of surgery at the Minneapolis VA, where a large number of surgical patients needed care that could be provided, in part, by our surgical residents. I discussed with Humphrey the possibility of the VA becoming affiliated with the University of Minnesota. As the current VA surgical residents finished their training, we would then rotate the University of Minnesota residents through the VA for that clinical exposure. The VA's patients had a wide variety of medical problems, including hernias, gallbladder disease, peptic ulcer disease, gastrointestinal cancer, peripheral vascular challenges, and lung cancer. I appointed Humphrey a vice chairman of the University of Minnesota surgery department; he also continued as chief of surgery at the VA.

I then approached Dr. John Perry at the Ramsey County hospital (now Regions Hospital) in St. Paul with exactly the same conditions that I had proposed to Humphrey at the Minneapolis VA. I knew that our surgical residents needed exposure to the field of trauma care, since they received virtually no such exposure at either the University of Minnesota's hospital or the VA. The Ramsey County hospital would provide our residents with good training in the surgical care of trauma patients. In addition, I suggested to Perry that University of Minnesota residents could eventually rotate through the Ramsey County hospital for general surgical training, not just trauma care. Perry accepted my ideas and we created a very successful Ramsey program affiliated with the University of Minnesota. I also appointed Perry a vice chairman of the University's surgery department; he, too, continued as chief of surgery at Ramsey.

I then approached Dr. Claude Hitchcock at what is now called Hennepin County Medical Center in Minneapolis with the same thought in mind that we could perhaps gain trauma care experience for our University of Minnesota residents at his hospital. Unfortunately, my visit with Hitchcock was not as successful as my visits with Humphrey and Perry. Hitchcock informed me that his program was independent and would remain so; he would continue to train general surgeons for the state of Minnesota, as he had done since he took over as chief of surgery at that institution. Apparently, Hitchcock was still quite upset that Wangensteen had not kept him on the staff at the University of Minnesota's hospital after he completed his residency. Therefore, he would not accept any affiliation whatsoever with the University of Minnesota. In many ways, his refusal to affiliate turned out to be a good decision on his part, since the state needed at least 1 surgical program producing community surgeons.

Looking further for trauma care training for our residents, I then approached the administrator of North Memorial where many of our residents were moonlighting. I found that we could have a rotation at North Memorial, which would provide us with additional trauma care training for our residents.

Finally, I felt that it was important to expose our residents to the private practice of surgery in the Twin Cities community. As they observed firsthand the life of a private practitioner of surgery, they could decide whether they truly wanted to remain in academic surgery or instead go into private practice. I spoke to several key individuals at what is now Park Nicollet Medical Center, a large private practice clinic in the western suburb of St. Louis Park that used the adjacent Methodist Hospital for surgical patients. One of the most gifted surgeons at Park Nicollet was Dr. Earl Yonehiro (who changed his surname to Young), one of the best surgical technicians to ever graduate from the University of Minnesota surgical program. He was delighted to have our residents rotate on his service, both at Park Nicollet and at Methodist. This proved to be one of the best rotations we could have had. The group of surgeons at Park Nicollet were happy to assist our senior residents as they emerged from 2 to 4 years in our research laboratories, offering them the chance to care for a large number of patients in need of common surgical procedures. Thus, at this point, in 1969, the University of Minnesota surgical training program was pretty well set.

Regarding routine weekly conferences for faculty and residents, the mortality and morbidity conference that Wangensteen had started was doing very well. However, only selected cases were being presented, rather than all complications that occurred on our surgical services. I therefore insisted that all complications, no matter how small, were to be listed and discussed at our weekly mortality and morbidity conference. Several faculty members were very upset by this request, worried that, if we had to present all of our wound infections and other minor complications, the weekly conferences would become long and boring. I countered that, if we had that many wound infections and other minor complications, they definitely needed to be discussed so that we could learn to prevent them in the future.

The weekly conference that I enjoyed most of all was Grand Rounds on Saturday mornings, so aptly described by Cohen as having "an atmosphere of competitive informality." I had never experienced rounds like these. At UCSF, surgeons presented cases, polite questions were asked, and the chief of surgery was the final arbiter on all surgical problems. In contrast, at Minnesota's Grand

Rounds, everyone would freely and fully bring up their own points. As department chairman, I found that my opinion was no more important than that of any other professor, resident, or even student who spoke up. These Grand Rounds, Minnesota-style, turned out to be the best teaching conferences I had ever attended. Visitors from other universities often walked away with the impression that we were a combative bunch. Yet at the completion of Grand Rounds, our social coffee breaks were quite amiable; in reality, most of us were close friends. Richard Lillehei, in particular, relished taking the opposite point of view on any Grand Rounds discussion. He was one of the primary sources of the intellectual interactions that occurred. He took delight in goading his favorite targets, Richard Varco and Michael Eisenberg. Lillehei's untimely death in 1981, at age 53, was a tragic jolt and a terrible loss.

One regular conference at Minnesota that I felt needed to be improved was our annual continuing medical education course, usually about 3 to 4 days long. The first time that I attended it, in 1967 before becoming chair, fewer than 100 surgeons were in the audience. An eclectic group of speakers would discuss breast cancer, then trauma, and then perhaps vascular surgery. It was easy to see how listeners could become less and less interested. The contexts and topics ranged too widely, without cohesive segues.

My first year as chairman, I reoriented the annual course to focus on a single subject and endeavored, from now on, to get the very best people in the country to give presentations on their specific expertise in that particular subject. To ensure clarity for our revitalized continuing medical education course, I chose 5 different subjects in surgery to rotate between: gastrointestinal surgery, hepatobiliary and pancreatic surgery, breast and endocrine surgery, trauma and critical care surgery, and vascular surgery. I at first simply encouraged our residents and students to attend and finally made it mandatory. I told them that by attending this course each year, they would learn in person from the very individuals who write the books and the journal articles on those crucial surgical subjects; they would hear back-and-forth debate on the very questions that tend to be asked in the national written and oral board examinations in surgery that all residents must pass. The popularity of our revamped annual course in surgery continued to grow, until, at one point, over 1,000 practicing general surgeons from throughout the United States and abroad attended. Even with a surge in similar conferences offered around the globe and on the web and with more convenient opportunities to obtain continuing education credits, our course still draws 300 to 400 attendees each year. We are frequently told that this course is the best surgical continuing education course in the country.

With the establishment of an organized residency program and the improvements in our weekly conferences and annual course, I was pleased with the structure now in place. Over the 40 years that I have been at the University of Minnesota, we have trained well over 200 academic surgeons: 20 of them became surgery department chairs at various universities, and another 50 or more became directors of surgical specialty divisions (such as critical care, vascular surgery, plastic surgery, and pediatric surgery). In addition, we have trained nearly 100 academic transplant surgeons who currently direct transplant programs throughout the United States and in many other countries. I feel that my strongest legacy will be these residents that I've had the privilege of training. For me, it's been a joy watching them progress academically and cheer them on as a friend and colleague as they, in turn, train others.

Chapter Thirteen
PANCREAS OR ISLET TRANSPLANTS

The brightest jewel in the crown of the Department of Surgery at the University of Minnesota is undoubtedly the story of our development of pancreas transplants as a possible cure for type 1 (insulin-dependent) diabetes. Because of the accomplishments in this area, the University of Minnesota has been referred to as the birthplace of pancreas transplantation.

As mentioned in Chapter Ten, when I visited the University of Minnesota in January 1967, I heard the exciting news about 2 diabetic patients who had just undergone pancreas transplants in December 1966. The first, a 28-year-old diabetic woman, received a duct-ligated segmental (partial) pancreas graft and a kidney graft from a deceased donor. Her operation on December 17, 1966, was performed by Dr. William Kelly. He used a technique devised by Dr. Frederick Merkel, a transplant fellow, who had tested the operation in dogs. In that first-ever human pancreas transplant, Kelly was assisted by Dr. Richard Lillehei. The pancreas graft was irradiated in an attempt to suppress the excretion of digestive enzymes like amylase. Unfortunately, irradiation did not work. The patient's course was complicated by a pancreatic fistula (an opening to the outside) that required open drainage of the amylase-rich pancreatic fluid. Both the pancreas graft and the kidney graft had to be removed on February 14, 1967, because of sepsis.

A second pancreas transplant was performed by Lillehei, with Kelly as his assistant, on New Year's Eve 1966. The 32-year-old patient received the entire pancreas graft, with its attached duodenum (the first part of the small intestine) brought out as a fistula in order to measure the graft's exocrine digestive function. Unfortunately, this patient died of an infection 4½ months after the transplant.

After my arrival as Department of Surgery chairman in the summer of 1967, I assisted on several pancreas transplants and became aware that it was too much of an operation for patients with brittle (uncontrollable) type 1 diabetes, as mentioned in Chapter Eleven. I therefore felt that we should return to the laboratory to find a more acceptable procedure for treating diabetes. In 1960, Dr. Arnold Lazarow, chairman of the University of Minnesota's anatomy department, had a special interest in the pancreatic islets of Langerhans (which contain the beta cells that make insulin). Graduate students working in his laboratory developed a technique to separate out the islets, which represent 2% of the entire pancreas (24). The islets could then be suspended in a solution after the acinar tissues (which secrete digestive hormones) had been separated out by the use of an enzyme called collagenase.

In the laboratory, I wanted to try to isolate islets as Lazarow had described, then inject them into diabetic rats to see whether or not doing so could cure their diabetes. A resident working in my laboratory, Dr. Edward Etheredge, began using Lazarow's technique to isolate rat islets. After 1 year, he returned to the clinical service. Another resident, Dr. David Sutherland (now a full professor here and director of our transplant program), entered my laboratory and continued this work, eventually isolating human islets as well as rat islets.

After successfully curing the diabetes of rats by injecting them with isolated rat islets, we felt we were ready to start treating human diabetic patients with isolated human islets, in an effort to cure their diabetes. We suspended human islets in a salt solution and eventually injected them directly into the patient's portal vein (which leads into the liver); thus, the injected islets would reside in the patient's liver (rather than pancreas), given the liver's dual blood supply (portal vein and hepatic artery). With this technique, we were able to reduce the total amount of insulin that diabetic patients were taking, but we never could achieve complete insulin independence in our first series of 7 human islet recipients. This nonetheless groundbreaking experience was presented to the international Transplantation Society in 1974 (25).

After those first 7 human islet recipients, we were concerned that perhaps our isolation of islets was somehow damaging the islets themselves. We needed to test the viability of the islets by transplanting them under conditions in which they would not be rejected. Thus, we chose patients who had pancreatitis (an inflammation of the pancreas that causes severe abdominal pain) who could only obtain relief by taking narcotics or having their inflamed pancreas removed. However, removing their pancreas would render them diabetic. To treat their diabetes, we decided to isolate each patient's own islets and return them back to that patient. Under this scenario, the islets should be readily accepted if they are viable. This procedure proved to be quite successful. Over 50% of our patients whose own islets were removed and then returned to them remained insulin-independent. Once again, serendipity came into play: a procedure designed to prove that the islets we prepared were viable proved to be an excellent treatment for patients with debilitating pancreatitis. We have now performed pancreatectomies for over 200 patients with pancreatitis; most were addicted to narcotics preoperatively and were eventually able to get off narcotics postoperatively.

We also determined that whole-organ pancreas transplants could be performed successfully with newer immunosuppressive agents that had become available in 1978. We began a series of clinical pancreas transplants once again. Some were performed simultaneously with a kidney transplant, as in the original mid-1960s series; others were performed as a pancreas transplant after the patient had already undergone a kidney transplant in the past. In addition, we began performing pancreas transplants alone for patients who were having serious complications of diabetes, but still had good kidney function. We developed techniques to determine when the patient's pancreas graft was in the initial phase of rejection so that treatment (with steroids and other immunosuppressive drugs) could be started to reverse the rejection process. We obtained whole-organ pancreas grafts from deceased donors, and also began transplanting part of a pancreas from living donors. These segmental (partial) living donors included siblings, parents, and even, occasionally, genetically unrelated individuals.

A landmark report from Dr. James Shapiro and colleagues of Edmonton, Alberta, Canada, appeared in 2000 in the *New England Journal of Medicine* (July 27, Vol 243, No. 4). In this report, Shapiro and colleagues described a unique protocol using a combination of new immunosuppressive drugs for islet recipients. They were able to achieve an excellent 2-year islet graft survival rate of 82%. However, their Edmonton program required islets from 2 or more human donors in order to achieve insulin independence for the recipients. Subsequently, we at the University of Minnesota developed a similar protocol with slightly different immunosuppressive drugs: we were able to achieve the same excellent results with a single-donor islet transplant. It was our thought that islet transplants would only be practical for treating a significant number of diabetic patients if we could use single donors. So we have continued to perform single-donor islet transplants in our diabetic patients.

In 2005, Shapiro and colleagues reported the 5-year follow-up results for their islet recipients, showing that insulin independence fell off after 5 years to less than 20% (26). Our own results at the University of Minnesota were slightly better, primarily because we gave a long-acting insulin preparation called Lantus to our recipients, in order to protect the islets from exhaustion in the early posttransplant period (with Lantus, the islets, at first, would only have to function after stimulation by meals). With this protocol, we were able to achieve a 50% rate of 5-year insulin independence. In both the Edmonton and our series, 80% of islet recipients after 5 years still had some islet function, as evidenced by having C peptide (the biologically inactive connecting amino acid) in their blood; such recipients, though not insulin-independent, were nevertheless protected from serious episodes of hypoglycemia.

Finally, we're now looking at the possibility of using pigs as a source of islets in order to obtain enough islets to treat the more than 1½ million patients with type 1 diabetes in the United States. A variety of protocols using different immunosuppressive drugs are being developed in our laboratory in order to transplant pig islets into humans. This research is ongoing at our diabetic institute, directed by Sutherland and Dr. Bernhard Hering. Hopefully, sometime in the not too distant future (3 to 5 years), we will be able to start a pilot series of transplanting pig islets into human patients with type 1 diabetes.

Of course, our goal in pancreas and islet transplants is to attempt to cure diabetic patients. As occurs with any new exploration in any field of medicine, many lessons are learned along the way. For example, placing transplanted kidneys in diabetic patients gave us an excellent opportunity to determine the earliest changes that can occur in a normal kidney when it is exposed to a diabetic milieu. However, one of the most important lessons we learned from our experience with pancreas transplants came from our series of identical-twin transplants. Typically, we transplanted a segment of the pancreas from the healthy twin to the diabetic twin. Since this was a transplant between identical twins, the graft would not be seen as a "foreign" tissue, so we did not need to use immunosuppressive therapy to prevent rejection. Unfortunately, in our first few transplants performed in this manner, within 4 to 6 months, the diabetic twin who had received the pancreas became diabetic again. In examining the transplanted pancreas, we found that the insulin-making beta cells in the transplanted pancreas had been destroyed by antibodies in the diabetic recipient. Thus, we were able to establish that antibodies are present in a type 1 diabetic patient against the beta cells that make insulin in the pancreas. This finding established the fact that type 1 diabetes is an autoimmune disease (27). In our subsequent transplants between a healthy twin and a diabetic twin, we used immunosuppressive therapy, just as we would between 2 individuals who are not twins. The pancreas transplants in twin recipients who were treated with immunosuppressive therapy successfully and permanently cured their diabetes.

The second type of diabetes is referred to as type 2 diabetes, present in 10 to 12 million patients in the United States. In this type of diabetes, the patient is capable of making insulin, but not enough insulin, since there is a degree of insulin resistance in the patient's body. Thus, they are relatively insulin-insufficient. Type 2 diabetes most often occurs in adults, specifically those with a genetic predisposition to it. Such patients are frequently obese; in some instances, they can be cured of their diabetes by losing weight (either by sticking to an appropriate diet or by undergoing bariatric surgery). Given the ongoing epidemic of obesity in the United States, we are now seeing type 2 diabetes even in overweight children. Type 2 diabetic patients of any age are candidates for a pancreas or islet transplant, specifically those who have episodes of hypoglycemic unawareness or suffer progressive secondary complications (such as blindness, amputations, or kidney failure).

Most of our attention regarding pancreas and islet transplants has been directed at patients with type 1 diabetes, the most lethal form. About 50% of type 1 patients who do not undergo a transplant will die of kidney failure; the remainder will die of vascular complications, including heart failure, stroke, and peripheral vascular disease (which can cause loss of an extremity, such as a leg or fingers or toes). And many type 1 diabetics eventually go blind. Neurologic complications also occur, with loss of sensation in the extremities or loss of normal bowel function. Tragically, very little can be done medically (as opposed to surgically) to help, other than attempting to regulate insulin levels. Even with the best results with insulin pumps and frequent blood monitoring, the progressive complications of type 1 diabetes are frustratingly difficult to control. But surgery in the form of a pancreas or islet transplant, if successful, is life-altering and even lifesaving.

If type 1 diabetic patients recognize the complications that can occur and, early on, pay close attention to regulating their blood sugar levels and to injecting insulin regularly, they might be capable of avoiding some of the complications, if fate smiles on them. I had a professor of endocrinology at the University of California, San Francisco (UCSF), who lived over 60 years with type 1 diabetes; from the onset of his disease, he carefully managed his blood sugar levels with multiple insulin injections and was able to escape most of the complications of his condition. But not everyone is so lucky. When a successful pancreas or islet transplant is performed, such patients are in fact cured of their diabetes.

Of note, insulin was discovered by 2 Canadians: Frederick Banting, an orthopedic doctor, and medical student Charles Best (28). It became the treatment of choice for diabetes for decades. Nowadays, with a successful pancreas or islet transplant, that recipient's diabetes is, in effect, cured. Pancreas or islet recipients who no longer have to check their blood sugar levels 4 times a day and no longer have to inject themselves with insulin 3 to 4 times a day, as they did in the past, frequently come to us and exclaim, "Thank you for giving me my life back!" Such patients are a joy to see and encourage us to continue our pursuit of ways to successfully treat more patients than we currently are able to. At the University of Minnesota, we now perform pancreas transplants in about 150 diabetic patients each year, which accounts for 10% of the 1,500 pancreas transplants performed each year in the United States. Our islet transplant numbers—currently about 25 each year with single-donor human islets as the source—will hopefully go up in the near future if our pig islet research yields results.

Chapter Fourteen
LIVER TRANSPLANTS:
THE JAMIE FISKE STORY

A liver transplant is probably the most technically demanding operation of all of the transplants that surgeons can perform. I consider our program at the University of Minnesota an active liver transplant program, with over 70 such transplants each year (over half using living donors). Our living donor liver program is the 2nd largest in the United States, but I realized how small our program is when I visited the mainland of China in 2007: in Beijing, at Tianijin First Central Hospital complex (a consortium of several hospitals), almost 700 liver transplants are performed each year. By comparison, the 2 busiest programs in the United States—the University of Pittsburgh and the University of California, Los Angeles (UCLA)—each perform about 200 liver transplants each year. The main reason for the high number in China is that a very large percentage of its population has hepatitis B and/or C, both of which can eventually lead to liver failure or liver cancer. Unfortunately, with increased drug use in the United States, hepatitis C is now increasing. Thus, I think, the number of liver transplants done here will continue to grow, assuming an adequate number of liver donors.

The reason a liver transplant is more technically challenging is that it requires at least 4 vascular (blood vessel) connections and 1 biliary tract connection to the intestine. The operation becomes even more complex with a living donor, since only 1 lobe (segment) of the liver is used, necessitating surgical closure of many bile ducts and vessels that extend between the lobes within the donor's liver. Every healthy liver has 4 lobes: the right (the largest), left, quadrate, and caudate lobes. The largest gland in the human body, the liver is the only organ that can self-regenerate (i.e., if part is removed, the remaining parts can frequently grow back to the original size and shape). The number of available deceased donor livers is quite limited in the United States. In China, however, the use of executed criminals as liver and kidney donors helps drive the large number of liver transplants performed in that country.

At the University of Minnesota, the first temporarily successful liver transplant was performed in 1964, when a 2½-year-old deceased donor's liver was placed into an 11-month-old infant with a condition called biliary atresia (lack of proper development of biliary ducts in the liver). This operation was performed by Dr. Karel Absolon, assisted by Dr. Richard Lillehei. It involved an add-on liver—a so-called heterotopic transplant, in which the recipient's own (native) liver is left in place and the new liver is implanted next to it. The liver graft functioned well for 13 days when, unfortunately, the child died of sepsis.

I began a formal liver transplant program at the University of Minnesota on July 2, 1968 (a year after I became chairman). Initially, our results were disappointing. But the program progressed, and by 1983, we were recording a patient survival rate of 20% at 3 years posttransplant. By 1993, we were able to achieve a patient survival rate of 60% at 3 years posttransplant and, finally, by 2003, a patient survival rate of over 80%. This increasing improvement in the patient survival rate was due primarily to improved surgical techniques, as well as improved immunosuppressive agents.

The darkest moment in our program's liver transplant history occurred in 1969 with our 5th liver transplant. The patient, a 43-year-old woman, was a graduate student in psychology at the University of Minnesota. She was seen in our student health clinic for vague gastrointestinal symptoms that persisted. Eventually, she became jaundiced and had what she described as a flu-like syndrome. Because of her jaundice, she was admitted to the hospital. Her condition continued to deteriorate, with progressively deeper jaundice and early kidney failure. All of her laboratory tests confirmed that her liver was failing rapidly. She was transferred to the transplant service, since her only hope for survival was a liver transplant. If an appropriate compatible donor liver became available, we would proceed with a liver transplant.

On June 18, 1969, a deceased donor liver became available. We performed a liver transplant under very difficult conditions: the lack of coagulation factors in the recipient's diseased liver resulted in major blood loss. She required close to 40 units of blood during the operation. Her native liver was noticeably shrunken, a finding that confirmed the diagnosis of acute yellow atrophy caused by viral hepatitis with massive hepatic necrosis. Posttransplant, she went into kidney failure and required dialysis. Unfortunately, after 2 weeks, she died as a result of multiple organ failure and sepsis.

After her liver transplant, 36 of us came down with hepatitis B, including doctors, nurses, and assistants in the operating room as well as laboratory and nursing staff members on the ward. Personnel from the Centers for Disease Control and Prevention (CDC) in Atlanta, Georgia, came to Minneapolis to review what had occurred; they made very helpful suggestions as to how to avoid a repeat of this type of calamity. We learned many lessons regarding how to handle blood and laboratory samples and how to improve our isolation techniques in the operating room, in the laboratory, and on the wards. I was among those 36: I became jaundiced and ended up home in bed with hepatitis for about 3 weeks before my condition improved enough that I could return to work. Once my blood tests for hepatitis were negative and I had developed antibodies to hepatitis, I was able to resume my surgical career.

After that low point in our liver transplant program, we implemented stringent safeguards and it became very successful. The highlight of the program was in 1982 with the riveting story of 11-month-old Jamie Fiske. She was born November 26, 1981, with biliary atresia, in an era when liver transplants had not been successfully performed in children under the age of 3. It was hoped that she could live long enough and grow sufficiently to eventually become a suitable candidate for a liver transplant.

Her father, Charles Fiske, of Bridgewater, Massachusetts, was a budget director for Boston University School of Medicine's department of psychiatry. He contacted me and wanted the transplant to be done at the University of Minnesota. In 1982, only 3 transplant programs in the United States had ever offered liver transplants to children, 1 of which had stopped doing so. Besides ours, the other remaining pediatric liver transplant program was at the University of Pittsburgh, whose staff had informed Jamie's father of a 3-week wait to evaluate her.

Since Jamie's condition was rapidly deteriorating, he chose to have her transplant done at the University of Minnesota. I told him on the phone that, if a suitable pediatric liver from a deceased donor became available, we would proceed with her transplant. He was delighted. He had Jamie transferred from Children's Hospital in Boston to our pediatric unit. Years later, he related to me that, after he and his wife, Marilyn, along with their other child, Daren, came to Minnesota, they wondered why they had come from the "medical mecca" of Boston to this hospital in the Midwest. While he was in the waiting room to have Jamie admitted, he had met 2 Native Americans from Fargo, North Dakota, who made it even more apparent that he was in the "wild" Midwest. He stressed he was so delighted when he and I met, because he appreciated that I had a very positive attitude and that I felt the transplant would be successful. Everyone up to that point had told him that it was unlikely this tiny 11-month-old could be successfully transplanted, since the youngest survivor reported by Pittsburgh's Tom Starzl was a 3-year-old.

I did not at first realize the full extent of Charles Fiske's ability and tenacity. He was bound and determined to find a deceased pediatric donor to supply a liver for Jamie. He began a very active campaign, which included telegraphing 500 pediatricians and sending a newsletter to the emergency room staffs of 1,000 hospitals. In addition, he contacted U.S. Senator Edward Kennedy and House Speaker Tip O'Neill, as well as CBS anchorman Dan Rather. With their help he was able to persuade the American Academy of Pediatrics to allow him to speak before the 1,000 academy members at their annual meeting in New York City on October 28, 1982. His impassioned plea at that meeting for a liver for Jamie ended with his repeating the words of his favorite song, "You Are My Sunshine," the last line of which is "please don't take my sunshine away." Everyone who heard him was emotionally moved.

His plea not only was heard by the pediatricians present at the meeting, but also was carried by hundreds of television stations and newspapers across the country. As he later stated, this vast media coverage was one of the many miracles regarding Jamie's case: it had been a slow news day so the story of an 11-month-old child dying of liver failure became the main news item. Over the next 7 days, about 500 families contacted us about Jamie, who was now waiting at the University of Minnesota hospital. Only 2 offers turned out to be useful. One, a liver from a 3-year-old on the East Coast, was not suitable for Jamie, but saved the life of an older transplant patient at Children's Hospital in Pittsburgh.

The second organ offer came from the father of a 10-month-old boy killed in a car-train collision in Utah. That father, Laird Bellon, had seen Charles Fiske on television and specified that his son's liver should go to Jamie. The decision to donate the boy's liver was made on a Wednesday. But it was Thursday before the physicians allowed Mrs. Bellon (who had sustained severe facial injuries in the collision) to leave her hospital bed in American Fork, Utah, for the 40-mile trip to see her son, who had been airlifted to Children's Hospital in Salt Lake City. After she had an opportunity to say an impassioned good-bye to her son, surgeons removed his liver and disconnected his life support system. With that, the couple returned to American Fork to await word of Jamie's surgery. "I hope the little girl makes it," Mr. Bellon said.

The Utah child's liver was flown to Minneapolis on Friday, November 5, 1982. We took Jamie to the operating room that same morning and removed her native, nonfunctioning liver. While the operation was progressing, at about 5:00 a.m., we were told that many members of the press were gathering in the lobby of the hospital. They had somehow been alerted to the fact that this now-famous patient was undergoing her liver transplant. Considering that no child under the age of 1 had ever successfully undergone a liver transplant, we were concerned that we might not be able to deliver good news to the waiting Fiske family and to the press.

But everything went very well, at first, during Jamie's operation. All of the blood vessel connections and the biliary tract connection were accomplished in an excellent fashion. I was fortunate to have 2 outstanding assistants: Dr. Nancy Ascher, currently the chair of surgery at the University of California, San Francisco (UCSF), my alma mater, and Dr. Peter Stock, now a liver transplant surgeon at UCSF.

However, when we had almost completed the operation, we discovered that the donor's artery leading to the newly transplanted liver could not reach the point where it needed to be connected with Jamie's main artery (her aorta). Would this be the Achilles' heel of this operation? After some discussion, we used a synthetic vascular graft to connect the hepatic artery to Jamie's aorta. Happily, everything again went very well. We were delighted to report the good news to her family and the press. Once again, it was my privilege as a surgeon to witness firsthand the miracle of transplantation: a miracle that never gets old for me.

Over the next few weeks, this little child who had recently been orange from jaundice, with a large protuberant belly filled with fluid secondary to her failing liver, gradually transformed into a normal-looking infant. Beginning about 2 to 3 weeks posttransplant, her skin color became normal. From that day forward, she continued to do well. She was discharged from the hospital on December 16, 1982, and was able to return home for the Christmas holidays.

Jamie continued to improve at home. About a year after her transplant, Charles Fiske was invited once again to speak at the American Academy of Pediatrics meeting, this time held in San Francisco. Marilyn Fiske, along with Daren and Jamie, also prepared to fly to San Francisco for the meeting. They decided to stop in Salt Lake City to see the Bellon family. They had been in contact with the Bellons all year with the continuing good news of Jamie's progress. When they arrived in Salt Lake City, both Daren and Jamie disembarked and began running down the airport corridor, at which time a pregnant Mrs. Bellon grabbed Jamie, held her up, and gave her a big squeeze. She turned to her husband and her parents and, with tears in her eyes, said "we made the right choice." It was an emotional meeting with hugs and kisses throughout.

The Fiskes continued their trip to San Francisco, where Charles spoke once again before the pediatric academy, this time accompanied by Marilyn, Daren, and Jamie. They received a standing ovation from the 1,000 pediatricians attending that meeting, whose approval of Charles Fiske's request to speak to them in New York the year before had resulted in the Gift of Life that Jamie received.

A lesser known aspect of Jamie's story is that Blue Cross-Blue Shield had first denied payment for her liver transplant. The insurance giant considered it experimental. Charles Fiske was able to persuade them to cover the procedure. Notwithstanding all of the publicity surrounding Jamie's case, it came down to the fact that Dr. Harvey Sharp, the pediatric liver specialist at the University of Minnesota, stated that we could not do her transplant if there wasn't insurance coverage. When this information was made public, Blue Cross rapidly reversed its earlier decision.

Jamie's case was instrumental not only in changing the attitude of insurance companies but also in inspiring the U.S. Congress to help make transplants happen. Charles Fiske testified before Congress at the request of Al Gore, then a representative, emphasizing that there must be a better way to distribute lifesaving organs than having to revert to the media. His testimony helped Gore in the House, and Orrin Hatch in the Senate, to pass the National Organ Transplant Act. This milestone legislation established a national Organ Procurement and Transplantation Network (OPTN) to develop a system of equitable allocation of donated organs. In addition, a national scientific registry was designed to compile and analyze data on all transplants performed and to suggest improvements to benefit transplant patients. President Ronald Reagan signed it into law in 1984. Eventually, in 1986, the United Network for Organ Sharing (UNOS) was awarded a federal contract to operate the national OPTN. Thus, in so many ways, Jamie Fiske's successful transplant affected organ transplantation in the United States.

Shortly after Jamie's transplant, reporter Claudia Wallis wrote an influential *Time* magazine (Nov. 22, 1982) article entitled "Which Life Should Be Saved?" She stated that the shortage of transplant organs raised many ethical questions. As an example, she told of a young Rhode Island patient named Justine Pinheiro who was still waiting in late November 1982 for a liver transplant, quoting her mother, Debbie Pinheiro, as admitting "we really get jealous over" all the media attention paid to Jamie's case. She and her husband tried to match Charles Fiske's efforts to focus attention on their daughter's need for a liver transplant. Wallis noted that they had "petitioned their Congressman and been headlined on the front page of the *Providence Journal,* in hope that 'the same thing that happened to the Fiskes happens to us.' " Sadly, their daughter died without ever receiving a lifesaving liver.

It would be another couple years before the National Organ Transplant Act would render it unnecessary for families to revert to publicity to obtain an organ for their loved one. In the meantime, given the Jamie Fiske case with its happy ending and the Justine Pinheiro case with its tragic ending, many ethicists began to discuss how such cases ideally should be handled. The American Medical Association (AMA) issued guidelines in 1984 stating that organs must be allocated to patients on a medical basis alone, reasoning that "social worth is not an appropriate criterion." Many other suggestions were made by ethicists, including the idea of a lottery to decide who receives an organ. In the Jamie Fiske case, however, 2 important facts must be kept in mind. Her parents, unlike others, had the resources to find a donor. And the donor family specified that the liver of their child should go to Jamie and to Jamie alone. Interestingly, at that time, 4 other babies in Pittsburgh were equally suited for a liver transplant but none had a greater medical need than Jamie. Moreover, even today, if a living donor (or the family of a deceased donor) wants to designate a recipient by name, then that's that: the donor's choice is final. (An exception is that so-called nondirected donors, who volunteer to give a kidney to a stranger, cannot designate a recipient.) In any case, the 1984 AMA guidelines that organs must be allocated to patients on a medical basis alone and that social worth is not an appropriate criterion were exactly what we followed back in 1982 when we accepted the Utah boy's liver for Jamie.

In the summer of 2006, while I was attending an international transplant meeting in Boston, I had the opportunity to see Jamie and her mother, Marilyn Fiske. At that meeting, 24 years after Jamie's liver transplant, she was a completely healthy young lady, a college graduate beginning a career as a teacher for preschool children. Although I had seen her on a regular basis in the first few years after her transplant, the intervals became longer and longer between her visits to Minneapolis, thanks to her continuing good health. I had always received Christmas cards and photos from the Fiskes with news of her progress, but had not seen Jamie in 7 years. Of course, we had continued to monitor her laboratory results and still will, as part of the routine follow-up our transplant program does. In Boston that day in 2006, Jamie, Marilyn, and I had a very nice visit. I was brought up-to-date on her older brother, Daren, currently enrolled in a program for holistic medicine and acupuncture in Whittier, California. Marilyn continues as a teacher, as always. Charles, who in 1988 started a transplant house for patients and their families in Boston called The Family Inn, is still involved with that program; in addition, he is currently the vice president of community and government relations with the Bamsi Company in Boston, a nonprofit human service agency that provides a wide scope of social services.

After Jamie Fiske's 1982 triumph, our liver transplant program at the University of Minnesota continued to grow, incorporating many technical improvements and modifications. We are now able to split a single deceased donor liver into 2 grafts, thus helping 2 different liver transplant recipients with 1 donor. We are also performing an increased number of living donor partial donor liver transplants.

Although the story of Jamie Fiske is one of sheer delight, the ethical considerations it spotlighted are still endlessly discussed by ethicists, internists, and surgeons at various meetings and in the media. What should the role of publicity be in focusing attention on an individual patient in need of a transplant? How much say should a living donor, or the family of a deceased donor, have in designating the intended recipient? Though organ allocation guidelines have been greatly strengthened since her 1982 transplant, the debate continues, even to this day. I have seen billboards that state the need for an organ for a specific person. Ads requesting an organ are placed in newspapers or in church bulletins. Many of these attempts have been successful. However, despite all efforts, over 100,000 patients are currently waiting in the United States for an organ transplant. Each day, 10 on that waiting list will die. Thus, the organ shortage remains a major problem that may only be solved if we can ever surmount the challenges associated with heterografts, also called xenografts (i.e., grafts from animals for human recipients), or if stem cell research someday allows us to grow new organs.

Nowadays, given the growing waiting list for organs, many patients with adequate funds go looking for organs from foreign countries. Pakistan is one of the most popular destinations for "transplant tourists" from Europe: the usual asking price for a kidney is $15,000, with the donor receiving only a 10th of that sum; much of the fee goes to middlemen or to the hospitals. In some villages in poor areas of Pakistan, almost no one has both kidneys, according to some reports. Transplant tourism still goes on in China, where 99% of organs come from executed prisoners, with an estimated 10,000 executions each year. The Chinese government says that organs are taken lawfully with the prisoner's consent, but this claim is impossible to verify. Transplant tourism accounts for about 10% of global transplants. Some theorists consider the Iranian system, in which living donors are routinely paid and well looked after and in which the supply of organs matches the demand, as a workable model or even the gold standard. We may eventually begin paying living donors in the United States—a hotly debated subject. If so, the Gift of Life would no longer be a gift.

Chapter Fifteen
THE JOY OF CHILDREN

When I arrived in Minneapolis in 1967, I was delighted to find that of the 75 kidney transplants that had been performed at the University of Minnesota, 29 were in children under the age of 16. At that time, given the general results for kidney transplants throughout the United States and abroad, only 10% to 15% of kidney transplants were performed in children. The much higher percentage (39%) in Minnesota was due to our excellent and quite active pediatric nephrology group. With the exception of one 18-month-old girl, all the children in the Minnesota series as of 1967 had been at least 7 years old at the time of their kidney transplant; thus, their body size was easily able to accommodate a kidney from an adult donor. For those 29 pediatric recipients, a total of 38 donor kidneys had been used (counting retransplants after some initial grafts failed). According to the world registry, the patient survival rate in 1966 was 45% at 1 year posttransplant and 38% at 2 years (29). The Minnesota pediatric kidney experience was essentially the same: a graft survival rate at 1 year posttransplant of 60% with living related donors and 30% with deceased donors.

I was delighted in 1967 with the experience that Minnesota already had with pediatric kidney transplants—among the most rewarding transplants that we can perform. Currently, we have now done over 950 kidney transplants in children, with a graft survival rate at 5 years posttransplant in excess of 90% using living donors.

Even with the already good results in 1967, it was apparent that very small children presented major problems, particularly infants under the age of 2 and most particularly those under the age of 1. The primary kidney disease in infants and children was typically secondary to poorly developed kidneys or to obstructive kidney disease. In the early 1970s, in infants under the age of 1, we attempted 4 transplants of bilateral deceased donor pediatric kidneys. In all 4 cases, the kidney grafts were eventually rejected. This experience made us aware that children are born with a mature immune system, allowing them to survive in the hostile environment that they're exposed to, including diseases resulting from bacterial or viral infections. Thus, the immunosuppressive agents available back then (including Imuran, prednisone, and antilymphocyte globulin [ALG]) were not adequate to maintain deceased donor organs in these small infants.

So, we felt we had to turn to living related donors. Most infants do not have siblings who are old enough to be used as living kidney donors. Therefore, their donors would have to be mothers, fathers, aunts, uncles, and sometimes grandparents. Given the discrepancy in size between an infant and an adult donor, we wrestled with the problem of implanting an adult kidney (which is about the size of an adult fist) into the abdomen of a small infant. Eventually, we developed surgical techniques for successfully implanting these large adult kidneys into infants under the age of 2. Amazingly, a large adult kidney rapidly adapts to the infant's body size, with decreased function at first; eventually, the transplanted kidney increases in function as the child grows—a really remarkable phenomenon.

Even today, most other transplant programs would prefer to wait until a child is at least 2 years old and represents a better size match for adult kidneys. However, we knew that infants under the age of 1 with chronic kidney failure often have severe growth retardation; in particular, the cranium does not grow appropriately, resulting in a smaller than normal skull. This condition, called microcephaly, can result in developmental delays and in a high incidence of central nervous system problems. And a smaller head size often results in mental development scores below the norm, with an intelligence quotient (IQ) below 100. For these reasons, we felt justified in wanting to transplant infants under the age of 1 if an adult living donor was available. For the first 17 infants under the age of 1 who underwent a kidney transplant at Minnesota, we measured their head circumference pretransplant and found the values to be significantly below the norm. But within 1 year

posttransplant, over half of the infants' heads were a normal size and
continued to grow normally. Moreover, after a successful kidney
transplant, most of their IQs approached 100 or more.

As we continued to develop better immunosuppressive
therapy for children, our results improved to the point where graft
and patient survival rates in children were often better than in
adults. By 1990, our living donor graft survival rate in children at 5
years posttransplant was in excess of 90%; patient survival, nearly
100%. For all children under 18, our graft survival rate at 5 years
posttransplant was about 85%.

Children with specific metabolic birth disorders posed a
challenge for us. One of the most difficult of these disorders is
oxalosis, in which the liver malfunctions; excessive oxalate crystals
are present throughout the body and are deposited in various
organs, affecting the kidneys in particular. Whenever we perform
kidney transplants in patients suffering from progressive kidney
failure, we give them medications to reduce the number of oxalate
crystals in the bloodstream. However, since the primary problem for
patients with oxalosis is in the liver, we began performing combined
liver and kidney transplants in their case. In later years, we were
able to obtain a patient survival rate of 100% at up to 5 years after a
liver transplant alone, if it was performed before kidney failure set
in. Oxalosis was one of the many inborn errors of metabolism that
we learned to correct with kidney transplants or with a combination
of kidney and liver transplants. Other metabolic birth disorders were
managed in a similar fashion.

Another problem posed by children with kidney disease was
the high number of conditions that could result in recurrence of the
primary disease posttransplant. We tried various techniques,
including subsequent transplants. In our series, recurrent disease
resulted in a loss of 4% to 6% of the kidneys transplanted in
children. An even higher graft loss rate was due to what is called
noncompliance or nonadherence: for one reason or another, often
due to unpleasant immunosuppressive side effects like puffy cheeks
(Cushing syndrome), children would stop taking their medications
posttransplant. Of the kidney grafts that were lost to rejection in our

pediatric transplant population, noncompliance was a factor about 50% of the time. In an effort to reduce the noncompliance rate, we adopted an immunosuppressive protocol that included rapid reduction of prednisone, since this steroid tends to result in some disfigurement, especially disturbing to young girls in our appearance-obsessed culture. Once we were able to reduce or eliminate the use of prednisone, our noncompliance rate markedly dropped.

Other significant refinements in our care of the pediatric kidney transplant population included an emphasis on preemptive transplants (i.e., performing the transplant before dialysis) and on reducing the number of blood transfusions pretransplant to under 5. This dual approach resulted in a general improvement in our kidney graft survival rates. In addition, our use of antibodies, such as ALG, to induce immunosuppression improved our graft survival rates as well. In recent years, our immunosuppressive therapy has gravitated toward tacrolimus and mycophenolate mofetil (CellCept), rather than cyclosporine and azathioprine (Imuran). Once again, this change also has improved our survival rates.

One of the real joys of transplanting children is how rapidly they become healthy. Despite such a large operation, on the first postoperative day, the child is typically up and acting quite normal. In stark contrast, children in the throes of kidney failure do not grow; as infants, they do not eat and frequently have to be fed by a gastric tube. Once they undergo a kidney transplant, they immediately blossom. They begin eating and are able at last to develop on track and catch up with their peers. No greater reward could a transplant surgeon hope to receive than these children's vibrant health. A tangible bonus comes when they send letters or cards (of which I have a drawerful) with invitations to their high school or college graduation ceremonies or their weddings. Every day I still count my blessings that I was fortunate enough to participate in the remarkable miracle of organ transplantation, from infancy on.

Chapter Sixteen
TRANSPLANT TRAINING
AND GENERAL SURGERY

In the past 3 chapters, I have outlined the role that the University of Minnesota has played in the development of pancreas and islet transplants (Chapter Thirteen); liver transplants, especially the Jamie Fiske story (Chapter Fourteen); and kidney transplants, with an emphasis on our 950 kidney transplants in children (Chapter Fifteen). The foundation of any program in transplantation is best measured by its accomplishments with kidney, liver, and pancreas transplants. Nonetheless, Minnesota has also significantly contributed to the success of other organ transplants and continues to do so today, both clinically and experimentally.

HEART TRANSPLANTS

It is not surprising, given our department's historic accomplishments in open-heart surgery (Chapter Four), that the godfather of heart transplantation, Dr. Norman Shumway, was trained at the University of Minnesota. Shumway was a resident at the University in the 1950s and worked with Dr. F. John Lewis, who, using hypothermia, performed the world's first open-heart operation on September 2, 1952. After finishing his surgical residency and obtaining his Ph.D. at the University of Minnesota in 1956, Shumway went into private surgical practice in Santa Barbara, California, and soon became bored. In an effort to find a university position, he was eventually hired by Stanford University in 1958 to establish a cardiovascular research program.

In 1959, while working with surgical resident Dr. Richard Lower, Shumway began to pursue his true interest: heart transplantation. Lower and Shumway began transplanting hearts between mongrel dogs, using what eventually became known as the

"Stanford technique." This simplified and shortened procedure led to survival rates of 60% to 70% in dogs. Shumway felt the procedure was ready to be applied in human patients.

Another surgeon who also trained in the 1950s at the University of Minnesota, Dr. Christiaan Barnard, heard that Shumway was ready to perform the first human heart transplant. So he came back from Capetown, South Africa, in October 1967 to learn the Stanford technique from Lower, who was now on the staff at the Medical College of Virginia in Richmond. When Shumway, in November 1967, formally announced that he was ready to perform a human heart transplant, Barnard quickly returned to South Africa, where he performed unsuccessful heart transplants in 40 dogs. Then, on December 3, 1967, Barnard performed the world's first human heart transplant. The recipient, Louis Washkansky, died a few weeks later of pneumonia.

Shumway performed the first successful heart transplant in the United States in January 1968, and continued to develop the surgical technique. Today, a patient undergoing a heart transplant has an 85% chance of surviving 1 year and a 70% chance of surviving 5 years. The current longest-surviving heart recipient, a Shumway patient, is doing well 28 years posttransplant.

At the University of Minnesota, we have performed more than 600 heart transplants. Shumway's daughter, Dr. Sara Shumway, is a professor of cardiovascular and thoracic surgery here and one of the directors of our heart transplant program.

LUNG AND HEART-LUNG TRANSPLANTS

We are also proud of our lung transplant program, which handles about 50 lung transplants each year. This pioneering program began in 1988, just 2 years after the first successful lung transplant was reported from Toronto General Hospital in Canada. Our Minnesota lung transplant program is currently the 4th most active in the world. One unique feature is that it is directed by an internist-pulmonologist, Dr. Marshall Hertz. All of our other solid-organ transplant programs are directed by surgeons. Hertz has focused on the use of living related donors as well as deceased donors. Our heart-lung transplant program began in 1986 with equally successful results.

INTESTINAL TRANSPLANTS

The University of Minnesota has also made major contributions to the development of intestinal transplants. In the early 1960s, Dr. Richard Lillehei's experimental studies of intestinal transplantation were the stimulus for opening this field to clinical endeavors. The world's first successful clinical intestinal transplant was credited to Lillehei and Dr. William Kelly in 1966, as part of the first pancreas transplant. With that first-ever pancreas graft came the deceased donor's duodenum (the first portion of the small intestine). Subsequently, most clinical pancreas transplants included a segment of the duodenum. Eventually, we at Minnesota began an intestinal transplant program, using isolated intestinal grafts as well as intestinal grafts combined with other abdominal organs. Dr. Rainer Gruessner continued our intestinal transplant program using only living related donors. A total of 10 segmental living donor intestinal transplants have now been performed at our institution.

STEM CELL TRANSPLANTS

Minnesota has played a very important role in the development of stem cell transplants. The world's first bone marrow transplant was performed here by Dr. Robert Good on August 27, 1968; the donor was a 5-year-old girl whose brother had immunologic deficiency disease. The recipient, David Camp, is now the father of twins. The stem cell transplant program at Minnesota is currently among the 5 most active in the United States, performing more than 200 transplants yearly.

FORMAL TRAINING

A key contribution to the overall field of transplantation was the establishment of formal training programs. In 1969, Dr. Richard Simmons and I set up a formal fellowship training program at the University of Minnesota. Initially, our program involved 6 months of training of what we called a donor doctor; responsibilities included placing all vascular access lines and shunts, as well as performing all of the donor operations (both deceased donors and living donors). During the second 6 months of the training program, the fellow would be responsible for kidney transplant recipients, either as a lead surgeon or a first assistant. As the numbers of pancreas and liver transplants increased, our training program was lengthened to 2 years, with 6 months as a donor doctor, 6 months as a kidney fellow, 6 months as a liver fellow, and 6 months as a pancreas fellow.

As the 4th president of the American Society of Transplant Surgeons (ASTS), my presidential address in June 1977 focused on the importance of education as a foundation for organ transplantation. Before that time, transplant surgeons were trained in a variety of ways—primarily on the job. I felt strongly that a formal training program, like the one we had developed at the University of Minnesota, would be crucial for our discipline's growth, in quantity and in quality. In my ASTS address, I stressed the importance of formal transplant training for surgeons who had completed surgical training and had qualified for the American Board of Surgery. I also stressed that comprehensive surgical training should be a prerequisite for transplant fellowship training. I felt that ASTS candidates should have completed, along with their national board examinations, a minimum of 1 year of formal transplant training. Preferably, that year of formal transplant training would be in a general surgery program, but urology was also acceptable given the prevalence of kidney transplants at that time.

Two years later, in his 1979 ASTS presidential address, Dr. James Cerilli reemphasized the importance of training that I had stressed in my address. He placed on my shoulders the responsibility of developing a quality program that would become the standard in the entire country. Specifically, he appointed me chairman of a newly formed education committee and put me in charge of evaluating and approving training programs at all U.S. institutions involved in clinical transplantation. Only approved institutions would be listed in the annual ASTS program book. Completion of training at an approved institution, along with high-enough scores on the boards in general surgery or urology, would be required for ASTS membership. The establishment of this formal training program was an extremely vital move for our young society to make. I'm happy that the ASTS took this initial step in 1979 and thus could avoid paternalism from the American Board of Medical Specialists.

I felt that transplant institutions seeking ASTS approval needed to submit a written application and undergo a site visit. In the first year, 18 institutions applied; 15 were eventually approved to offer a 1-year formal transplant fellowship. I continued to chair the education committee through 1988. Since then, it has been gratifying to see continuing progress under the leadership of Dr. Nancy Ascher and eventually Dr. Peter Stock. Both Ascher and Stock were trained at the University of Minnesota and are now at one of my alma maters, the University of California, San Francisco.

Currently, the ASTS has accredited 67 transplant programs: 63 in the United States (including Puerto Rico) and 4 in Canada. By organ, the numbers are as follows: 13, kidney alone; 24, kidney and liver; 4 kidney and pancreas; 3, liver alone; and 23, kidney, liver, and pancreas. In order to receive ASTS accreditation, an institution must provide adequate transplant volumes. The current standards are 60 kidney transplants per year, 50 liver transplants per year, and 20 pancreas transplants per year. In order to receive a certificate of completion at the end of a 2-year fellowship, a fellow must have performed, or been the first assistant on, a minimum number of transplants of each organ that the program is accredited in (30, kidney; 45, liver; 15, pancreas).

With the continuing development of approved transplant programs and the rigorous training of transplant surgeons and physicians for the future, growth in the field of solid-organ transplantation is assured. The primary limit to success remains the shortage of donor organs. As mentioned earlier, ongoing research on xenotransplants and stem cells will hopefully resolve the organ shortage problem in the not too distant future.

GENERAL SURGERY

For the most part, I was very pleased with the development of the transplant fellowship program, both at Minnesota and then via the ASTS. However, as time progressed, it became more and more apparent that trainees would be hired by academic programs for 1 type of operation only, namely, transplants. It was my hope, since transplant fellows had already been fully trained in general surgery, that they would continue to be general surgeons, albeit with specific research and clinical skills in transplant surgery. However, the current trend in medicine today is toward highly specialized training in specific areas. This trend applies to internists and to most other physicians as well. It is difficult today to find any surgeons who are as competent in general surgery as most surgeons were in past eras. Our graduates in surgery nowadays almost always spend 1 or 2 years as fellows in an array of specialties (transplant surgery, cardiovascular disease, oncology, colorectal surgery, infectious disease, critical care, endocrinology, plastic surgery).

As I look back on my career, one of my main reasons for leaving Scripps Clinic and Research Foundation in La Jolla was my desire to practice general surgery, as I had been trained to do. In addition, of course, I wanted to develop transplant surgery as my area of specific competence. I was hoping that my own trainees could follow this same road. I derived as much professional satisfaction from my general surgical practice (which amounted to 60% to 70% of my clinical activity) as I did from my transplant specialty.

My general surgical practice included oncology, surgical endocrinology, peptic ulcer disease, colorectal disease, appendectomies, complex and simple hernia repairs, and complicated hepatobiliary and pancreatic surgery. In addition, I very much enjoyed vascular surgery as well. In my general surgical practice, I was fortunate to take care of patients from almost every walk of life. This made for a rich professional and personal experience. I vividly recall many of these patients whose medical problems provided joy and sometimes sadness, both of which we would share together.

On my short list of the most admired individuals that I had the pleasure of caring for is former Vice President Hubert Humphrey. Unfortunately, Humphrey had bladder cancer, which spread to surrounding tissues. Eventually, his condition required an oncology specialist for his continuing care. He returned from Washington, where he was again serving in the United States Senate, to Minneapolis where he was under the care of Dr. B.J. Kennedy, the head of oncology at the University of Minnesota. As time progressed, it became evident that Humphrey would need surgery to control the spread of his tumor. Kennedy asked me to see Humphrey and to take care of him surgically. I eventually operated on him and had the privilege of taking care of him, in collaboration with Kennedy, for the remaining 6 months of his life.

While Humphrey was in the hospital, there was a real concern about his privacy. The University provided security so that he would not be bothered by uninvited visitors or by anyone seeking an autograph or photo op. The most interesting security usually came on days when no one seemed to be in the hall on the surgical floor. Once, I stepped outside of Humphrey's suite of rooms and saw a man at each end of the hall and another in front of the elevator, each wearing an earpiece and dressed in a 3-piece suit. It was obvious that this was Washington's Secret Service: I then knew that Vice President Walter (Fritz) Mondale, a frequent visitor, was coming to Minneapolis to see his friend. It was always such a pleasure to see Fritz Mondale, one of many great fans of Humphrey.

To be Humphrey's primary physician as he approached the end of a most remarkable life was an unbelievable honor for me. This man had so poignantly stated, "our progress as a nation could be judged by how we treat those in the dawn of life—the children;

those in the shadows of life—the poor, the jobless, and those who suffer from prejudice and discrimination; and those in the twilight of life—the elderly and those in poor health"(30). Truly he believed this statement; his record in the Senate in particular reflected this philosophy. He jointly sponsored Medicare in 1949, the Commission on Civil Rights in 1949, the Civil Rights Act of 1964, the establishment of the Peace Corps in 1960, the creation of the Job Corps in 1949, and the establishment of the Head Start program in 1951. These landmark laws, along with many others, remain profound legacies of the action-oriented philosophy of this most unusual, most decent gentleman. Our many conversations left me in awe of him.

Eventually Humphrey became well enough to return to his nearby Waverly, Minnesota, home. Kennedy and I continued to treat him as an outpatient. For the residual tumor in his pelvis, he underwent radiation and chemotherapy. One day I said, "Hubert, we've done about as much for you as we can for awhile. Why don't you go back to Washington where you want to be?" Humphrey replied, "Doctor, that is good advice."

He then returned "home" to the Senate to let his life pass before him in airbrushed glory. President Jimmy Carter delivered him to Andrews Air Force Base aboard Air Force One. The Senate convened a Special Session to welcome him back and to praise him. The full Senate chamber greeted him with 5 minutes of steady applause as he entered. A week later, the House of Representatives broke a 189-year tradition by inviting a member of the Senate to a Special Session in his honor: a huge official love feast for Humphrey. He spoke to the House members, standing where the President of the United States gives the State of the Union Address. Breaking into a wide grin, he gushed "myyy goodness." He later told me that riding on Air Force One, visiting Camp David for the first time, and standing where the President gives the State of the Union Address were all dreams come true.

The House tribute rounded out the official leave-taking from the big 3: the President, the Senate, and the House. But the best was yet to come: a dinner at the White House where Frank

Sinatra sang one of Humphrey's favorites, "The Lady Is a Tramp." Elizabeth Taylor, the new jewel of Washington glitter, kissed him on each of his sunken cheeks. The Treasurer of the United States, a black woman named Azie Taylor Morton, got up and said "were it not for Hubert Humphrey, I might not be here tonight without an apron on" (30). What a wonderful tribute to this most extraordinary man.

Humphrey eventually returned to Minneapolis and to his Waverly home. We arranged to have his medical care continued at this home, with round-the-clock nursing care and weekly visits by Kennedy or me. During these remaining months, he was in truth "the happy warrior." He looked on the positive side of everything. If, for one reason or another, we saw him at night, he awoke with the same positive attitude that he espoused during the day. I was so fortunate to have conversations with him during these months regarding the philosophy of life as he saw it. A most remarkable man!!!

Humphrey was just 1 patient out of many over the course of my general surgical career. Some were famous, some were infamous. Again, it makes me sad that our trainees today do not have the multilayered experience of caring for a cross-section of patients with a variety of treatable and, unfortunately, sometimes untreatable conditions. All of these patients enriched my professional life in ways that I will always be grateful for.

Chapter Seventeen
PERIPATETIC TRAVELS

Many challenges face a new chairman of a surgery department that can influence his success in that position. One relentless challenge is the constant call by the university administration to attend numerous meetings on curriculum, space, budgets, and general issues pertaining to all medical school departments. As I began my chairmanship, at least in the first year, I attempted to attend each and every one of these meetings. Interestingly, all of the nonsurgical services were always well-represented at the meetings and thus had a stronger voice in medical school affairs than the surgical services. At the conclusion of my first year, I determined which of these meetings were absolutely essential for me to attend and which I could send a member of my department to as my surrogate. This determination immediately reduced the number of meetings I personally attended by 70%.

The next most demanding challenge to my academic focus was work-related travel. Offers to speak elsewhere and to participate in far-flung conferences and meetings come very insidiously and are quite tempting. Travel itself is addicting, as it presents the opportunity to go to many places and see new things and meet new people. As chairman of a large surgery department, wherever I went, I was treated in regal fashion. As an example, I have been a visiting professor at over 60 medical institutions worldwide. At those institutions, my hosts did everything in their power to make my visit as pleasant as possible, including luxurious accommodations and fancy banquets. For the most part, they wanted me to stay for several days to teach their medical students and to interact with their residents and surgical staff, in addition to presenting a lecture or 2. I had to be very careful: most institutions wanted me to stay for 3 or 4 days. I made it a rule never to stay for more than 24 to 36 hours, except under very special circumstances. One such exception was my visiting professorship at Beth Israel Hospital in Boston in 1970: at the behest of my former fellow resident, Dr. William Silen, then its chairman of surgery, I accepted a stay of 3½ days. The primary reason for trying to keep all my trips as short as possible was to always be present at my own department's key weekly conferences, namely, our Mortality and Morbidity Conference and our Saturday-morning Surgical Grand Rounds.

Of course, my visiting professorships were often very pleasant and rewarding experiences. I always came back with new information that could be applied to my own department. In addition, in my own interaction with other institutions' medical students and residents, I could surreptitiously recruit outstanding graduates for our own surgical program. One thing I learned <u>not</u> to do was to ever perform surgery at an outside hospital. Once, as a visiting professor at Massachusetts General Hospital, I assisted a resident in performing a gallbladder removal. I returned home the next day, but eventually heard that our patient had a minor complication that I was powerless to help out with—a dilemma that would not have occurred if I had stuck to my own operating room.

Since I rarely went on a trip for longer than a day or so, my wife, Mignette, usually did not accompany me. But in 1970, 3 years after arriving in Minnesota, I was invited, along with a small group of senior surgeons, to Moscow and St. Petersburg (then called Leningrad)—the first time that a medical group from the United States was invited to travel behind the Iron Curtain. Since I would be gone for 5 to 6 days on this unique trip, Mignette decided to accompany me. We took our 2 oldest sons, Jon and David, who were 12 and 10 years old at the time. We all had a wonderful experience. We had a chance to visit several Soviet medical facilities, which, unfortunately, were quite archaic. American and English medical literature was not permitted in Russia at that time, so they were practicing medicine as it was practiced some 20 to 30 years earlier. The doctors there were extremely anxious to hear from us regarding our current surgical practices. I was glad I had brought along a few surgical texts, which were happily received by our hosts.

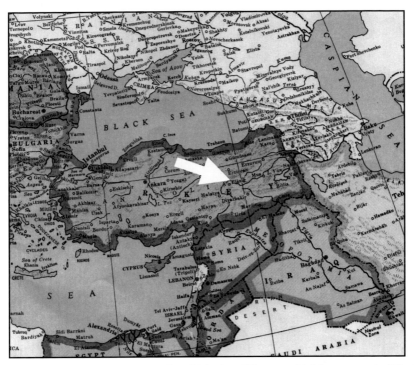

The site of the ancient Armenian and Turkish city of Harput, which became part of Elazig (*arrow*) in 1915: the birthplace of John Najarian's ancestors on both his father's side (the Najarians) and his mother's side (the Demirjians)

The car of John Najarian's parents in the 1930s: a bright red Flint

John Najarian at the
age of 6 on a pony

John Najarian, as a left tackle
(number 78), on the University of
California, Berkeley, football team

78 NAJARIAN, T

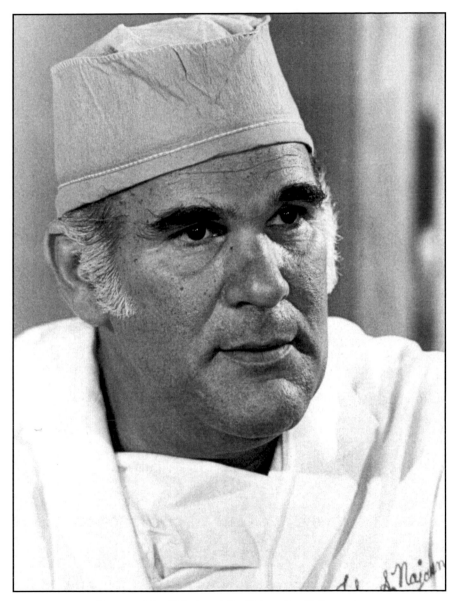

Surgeon John Najarian at the University of Minnesota

At St. Mary's Hospital in San Francisco in 1965

The University of California, San Francisco (UCSF),
campus on Mount Parnassus (now Sutro)

John Najarian (*middle row, 4th from the left*) and colleagues in 1963 at the Scripps Clinic and Research Foundation, La Jolla, California

John Najarian at his University of Minnesota desk in 1975

John Najarian with Owen Wangensteen (*right*), the University of Minnesota Department of Surgery chairman from 1930 until Najarian's arrival in 1967

John Najarian in London in 1987 as a new Honorary Fellow in the Royal College of Surgeons of England, shaking the hand of Sir Ian Todd (*left*), with Sir Roy Calne looking on (*far right*)

John Najarian with pioneering cardiac surgeon Michael DeBakey (*left*) of Houston, Texas

John Najarian greeting Pope John Paul II (*left*) in 2000

Jamie Fiske (with her mother, Marilyn Fiske, behind her) and John Najarian in 1986, at the 75ᵗʰ anniversary celebration of the University of Minnesota hospital

John Najarian with Jamie Fiske in 1985, at her routine evaluation 3 years posttransplant

John Najarian throwing the first pitch for the San Francisco Giants

On the farm near Benson, Minnesota, where Mignette Anderson Najarian grew up: John Najarian in 1960, flanked by 2 of her sisters, Patty Lou (*left*) and Claudette Ann (*right*)

John Najarian driving his boat on the St. Croix River (between Minnesota and Wisconsin)

John and Mignette Najarian, surrounded by 3 of their sons and daughters-in-law, at the November 2007 dinner celebrating the Najarian Endowed Chair

John and Mignette Najarian on vacation in Hawaii

John and Mignette Najarian with their 4 sons in front of their Minneapolis home: Mom and 5 football players

John Najarian bedecked with a pair of medals, for his Regents Professorship and his Endowed Chair—the 2 highest honors given to University of Minnesota faculty

Our sons had heard before we left home that Russian youth did not have chewing gum and would trade military medals for them. Thus, we brought many packages of chewing gum with us to Russia. Jon and David gave a stick of chewing gum to numerous Russian children in exchange for a variety of medals that they wore. One medal in particular was quite large, so the boys gave it to me to wear on my coat. It had to be extremely important because, with this medal on, every door was opened wherever we went. Thanks to that medal, we went to a very exclusive Russian circus and had excellent seats.

Moscow was a beautiful city. The streets were immaculate; no one would dare litter, for fear of being severely punished. When we went to see Lenin's tomb in Red Square by the Kremlin Wall, again with my large medal on, we were placed in the front of the line. We went through without having to wait the 3 or more hours that was typical in that line, which extended for blocks. Every morning, hundreds of Russian citizens waited to view his body. Lenin was preserved in lifelike form. Supposedly, Russian undertakers "rejuvenate" the body annually.

Ironically, the most picturesque parts of Moscow were the subway stations. They were really like art galleries, with exquisite statues and paintings in each station.

Of course, St. Petersburg was an absolute delight to see, particularly the Winter Palace (the winter residence of the Russian tsars) and the Hermitage Museum. One of the largest museums in the world, the Hermitage features 3 million works of art. The collections are displayed in 6 buildings, the main one being the Winter Palace. The art collection was breathtaking, even for our young sons.

Although I no longer wore that seemingly magical Russian medal back home in Minnesota, I always wore 2 hats as chairman of the surgery department: 1 as a surgeon, the other as a transplant surgeon. Obligatory trips for a department chairman were many, in particular, thanks to the 6 years that I was a member of the American Board of Surgery (ABS). My responsibilities as a board member included examining, 3 to 4 times per year, graduating surgical residents throughout the United States who were sitting for their Boards (i.e., taking 3 grueling half-hour oral examinations in order to be certified in general surgery). In addition, I attended most of the national and international surgical meetings, either to give presentations or to hear current surgical advances. For the same reasons, I would also attend transplant conferences in the United States and abroad.

After stepping down in 1993 as chairman, my travel obligations did not decrease, but actually increased, as I began accepting invitations to visit many of our 85 former transplant fellows. Minnesota transplant fellows who finished our training program now work in almost all European countries, including England, Spain, France, Denmark, Germany, and Greece.

One such trip I recall vividly was to Nicosia, Cyprus, in 1996 to visit former Minnesota transplant fellow Dr. George Kyriakides, who ran a small transplant program there. My arrival in Nicosia was heralded in the local newspaper. An Armenian girl who had been waiting for a transplant saw my name and asked Kyriakides if it would be possible for me to perform her transplant, with her mother as the living kidney donor. I hesitated, but eventually agreed to do her transplant. I learned another crucial lesion: back home in Minnesota, I was surrounded in the operating room by a surgical resident, a transplant fellow, a medical student, and, usually, 2 nurses. In stark contrast, in that small private hospital in Nicosia, I was working with a single individual. My only assistant was not a surgeon or a nurse, but had received some training as a surgical technician. Kyriakides performed the donor operation in another room under similar conditions. Luckily, the transplant went well, but it was extremely difficult. There was a slight language barrier: even the names of the instruments were different. I ended up performing the operation myself from the very beginning to the end (something I seldom ever did). I decided, once again, that I would never do surgery outside of my own institution, unless it was an emergency or unless I had been asked to demonstrate a new surgical or transplant technique.

Another particularly memorable trip was to Taiwan in 1997 to visit 2 former Minnesota transplant fellows from there. Since this trip would be for 6 days, Mignette accompanied me. Taiwan is a fascinating country, and the museum in Taipei is second to none. When Chiang Kai-shek's 1949 attempt to eradicate the Chinese communists in the mainland failed, he was forced to relocate his government in Taiwan, where he continued as president of the Republic of China (ROC) until his death in 1975. On fleeing mainland China, he took many glorious artifacts, statues, and artwork, all now displayed in the National Palace Museum in Taipei. One of the largest collections of Chinese marvels in the world, it has so many art pieces that the entire display is changed every 4 to 5 months.

Mignette and I proceeded to mainland China and had an opportunity to see Beijing. We found the streets filled with bicycles. Its air was polluted with smog from burning wood, used for heat in the umpteen individual homes and shacks on the outskirts. In downtown Beijing, however, several Swiss hotels that had just been completed were stunning and modern. Yet, whenever we left our hotel, we immediately arrived in an area of shacks, surrounded by unfortunate individuals, even women with infants in their arms begging for money. It was a sad sight. We did enjoy many of the local attractions in Beijing, such as the Great Wall, Tiananmen Square (built in the Ming Dynasty), and the Forbidden City, which houses the Palace Museum. We also toured the Summer Palace and its Garden of Nurtured Harmony, with the gorgeous artificial Kunming Lake and the famous Marble Boat. All in all, we were dazzled by the many magnificent tourist attractions.

A decade later, in 2007, I returned to Beijing to give several lectures at the Chinese National Transplantation meeting. The Beijing I found at that time was amazingly changed. The streets were now 8 lanes wide, highrise skyscrapers were being built everywhere, and I spotted only a few bicycles—instead, it seemed everyone had a car. One million Chinese had been displaced out of Beijing, in order to convert it to a modern metropolis in preparation for the 2008 Olympics. This transformation covered up the widening gap between China's mostly urban rich and its mostly rural poor. The average city dweller earns 3.3 times as much as his or her fellow citizen in the countryside. Regrettably, the communist party is spending money on a military buildup rather than on health care or education in the rural areas. I wonder how long the current ruling party will survive.

Other travels over my more than 40 years at the University of Minnesota were for the pleasure of accepting 5 honorary doctorates (University of Athens, Greece; Gustavus Adolphus College in St. Peter, Minnesota; California Lutheran College [now University] in Thousand Oaks; honorary fellowship in the Royal College of Surgeons, London, England; the University of Madrid). My foremost honor was being elected to the Royal College of Surgeons in London. I was particularly thrilled to receive the honorary fellowship in the Royal College, since it represents recognition by international surgeons. I was also pleased to be there with my longstanding friend Sir Roy Calne, who I believe was my sponsor. A heady bonus was touring the Royal College and seeing the memorabilia of all of the famous British surgeons of the past.

As a special treat, I flew back home from London on the Concorde, an incredible experience. The seats in the Concorde, only 2 on each side, were no bigger than what would be considered "coach" seats in most airplanes. The peculiar part was that smoking was allowed on 1 side, but not on the other side, just across the aisle. The aisle was barely 6 feet tall, with almost no room for overhead storage. These features made for a certain inconvenience, but it was the way construction had to be. In front of each seat was a plasma display screen showing our altitude: we climbed to 60,000 feet (all other commercial flights seldom exceed 42,000 feet). The screen also showed our air speed, which exceeded Mach 2.2 (over 1400 mph). Another intriguing feature was that the turbojet Rolls Royce engines were turned off as we passed over Windsor Castle, out of respect to the queen. The loud thrust sound of takeoff suddenly went to a deadly silence! If someone didn't know that the sudden silence was coming, it would be frighteningly eerie. Even I wondered whether or not the engines would start again, but they did. The whole trip from London's Heathrow Airport to New York's JFK was quite short (3.5 hours), so there was no time for a movie and hardly time to read more than the newspaper. The time schedule (thanks to such quickly passed-through time zones) actually indicated that we arrived before we had left. That short but riveting return trip was a once-in-a-lifetime experience. Sadly, the Concorde is no longer in use.

On top of the Royal College fellowship, I have also savored the somewhat less majestic but also deeply meaningful honor of being elected president of 3 world-renowned surgical societies, among others. I had also served as president of various national transplant societies and national surgical societies, but the pinnacles were presiding over the American Surgical Association (ASA), the international Transplantation Society (TTS), and the International Pediatric Transplant Association (IPTA). Each of these presidencies represented the highest recognition achievable in that field. These accolades came late in my career, so that my wife and our now-grown sons were able to accompany me to wondrous venues.

The first of these 3 presidencies came in 1989 with my election as the 108th president of the ASA [American Surgical Association], considered the granddaddy of all surgical societies in the United States. Its annual meeting that year was held April 10-12, in Colorado Springs, Colorado, at the Broadmoor Hotel. This site was nostalgic for me: it was the very same hotel where I had been successfully examined back in 1962 to become a Markle Scholar in academic medicine. Although I was excited to preside over the ASA meeting, I was also anxious to have an outstanding speaker for the final gala dinner.

I remembered that Dr. Bert Dunphy, my former surgery chief at the University of California, San Francisco (UCSF), had nabbed Dwight Eisenhower as the after-dinner speaker in 1961, when Dunphy was ASA president. Many members often spoke of the scintillating experience of seeing and hearing Ike. Since his speech, the after-dinner speakers had been far more ordinary. I felt that a standout speaker would make my ASA presidential meeting unforgettable for the members. I recognized that President Ronald Reagan's second term was to expire in January 1989 and that his wife, Nancy, was the stepdaughter of Dr. Loyal Davis, the chief of surgery at Northwestern Hospital in Chicago and himself a past ASA president (in 1956). I thought perhaps I could persuade Mrs. Reagan to land President Reagan as our after-dinner speaker for the meeting in Colorado Springs in April 1989. I repeatedly received messages that things looked good and that the President would be able to be our after-dinner speaker; however, just a month before the meeting, I received a memorandum from his secretary. It stated that Reagan would not be able to come to Colorado Springs to give the after-dinner talk, since he had committed to a speaking engagement for the same time in Japan. Thus, I was desperate to find a last-minute but preeminent speaker for the ASA gala dinner.

After thinking of various possibilities, I felt the best individual that I might possibly persuade to come would be NBC news anchor Tom Brokaw. I had known Brokaw since we lived in California, when he was the co-anchor of television station KNBC in Los Angeles, along with Tom Snyder. Brokaw had come to San Francisco to film a documentary on transplantation when I was the chief of transplantation at UCSF. He and I had become friends, primarily during the 3 to 4 extended visits needed by him and his film crew. Now, more than 2 decades later, it was with some trepidation that I called him and told him of my predicament. I asked him if there was any possibility that he could come to Colorado Springs to give a talk to the senior surgeons of the United States. I had some hope since his father-in-law, brother-in-law, and sister-in-law were all doctors. But he had the NBC nightly news to do; I feared that it was unlikely I could persuade him to give the ASA talk. To his credit, after some hesitation, he said "yes, I will do it, I will come to Colorado Springs." He gave an absolutely mesmerizing after-dinner presentation, touching on his unique experiences with various world leaders such as Fidel Castro, Mikhail Gorbachev, and, yes, President Ronald Reagan. Brokaw shared compelling stores about each. Both informative and entertaining, his talk is generally considered the most extraordinary after-dinner speech ever given to the ASA (31). To this very day, ASA members remember the meeting in Colorado Springs primarily because of Brokaw.

My own presidential address at that same ASA meeting in April 1989 was entitled "The Skill, Science, and Soul of the Surgeon," invoking the 3 legs of the stool so vital for a good surgeon (32). First and foremost is technical skill, often referred to as the craft of surgery. In fact, the word surgeon is derived from the Greek term for "the art of working with the hands." The second leg of the stool of surgery is science, which involves the continuing advance of research—the most significant way for surgery to continue to progress. Finally, and perhaps paramount, is the soul of the surgeon. As I said in my address, "Once the components of skill and science become the essential embodiment of the surgeon, it means little if the moral fiber is not there." I pointed out that "through the years, physicians have continued to distance themselves from their patients.... And yet, the simple act of holding a patient's hand can emphasize the compassion that could help transcend the current criticism of modern medicine." Even when I read the published version of my address today, I would not change a word. While in Colorado Springs with me that lovely April, my family enjoyed trips to Pikes Peak, the Garden of the Gods, and the Air Force Academy (especially the Air Force Chapel), as well as the many sporting activities available at the Broadmoor Hotel, such as horseback riding, skeet shooting, and fishing.

My second major presidency, of TTS [The Transplantation Society], culminated in August 1996 at the annual meeting in Barcelona, the second largest city in Spain and the capital of Catalonia (bordering France and the Mediterranean Sea). Barcelona is one of the most gorgeous cities in the world. Founded as a Roman city, it has a rich cultural heritage. Its enviable position on the Mediterranean makes it a tourist magnet. My family and I were captivated by the vivid designs of architect Antonio Gaudí, notably Güell Park and the Sagrada Familia.

As the 17th president of TTS, during its 30th anniversary, I felt it was worth reviewing the past 30 years in my presidential address, entitled "The Making of the Transplantation Society"(25). I spoke about the history of the development of genetics, histocompatibility, transplant immunity, clinical techniques, and immunosuppression. I speculated about the future of xenotransplantation and stem cell research. In those first 30 years, the society had grown from 200 members to over 2,000 members. Transplantation was now recognized as one of the most important medical advances of the 20th century. In my address, I lauded the Barcelona meeting, pointing out the remarkable work done by the local organizing committee in providing for our 3,400 registrants.

One of the highlights of the meeting was hearing the magnificent voice of one of the world's greatest tenors, Josep Carreras. He had been near death, suffering from lymphatic leukemia, just 6 years before. Thanks to a bone marrow transplant in Seattle, Washington, Carreras was not only well but obviously very healthy and in full voice. Because of a fire, his concert had to be moved from the splendid Barcelona Opera House to the much smaller Tivoli Theatre. However, he graciously agreed to give 2 performances to be sure that all of our registrants were accommodated. It was a Herculean effort to deliver back-to-back concerts; he even sang 3 encores after the second performance, which ended well after midnight.

Another highlight of the Barcelona meeting was that Lady Jean Medawar, widow of Nobel laureate and transplant giant Sir Peter Medawar, presented the Medawar Prize to the 3 recipients that year, Drs. Jean Dausset, Paul Terasaki, and Jon van Rood. To top it all off, we went to a sparkling amusement park called Tibidabo, along the lines of Disney World or the mythical Land of Oz, giving us a chance to relive our childhood. At Tibidabo, located on a mountaintop overlooking all of Barcelona, we relished junk food, good food, easy rides, and scary rides. All in all, the meeting was a huge success.

My third major presidency came in 1998, when I was elected the first president of the IPTA [International Pediatric Transplantation Association]. The meeting that I presided over was held in Venice in August 2000. Venice, I think, is everyone's favorite city. Situated on the Adriatic Sea, it was a trading center for both the Byzantine Empire and the Muslim world. With its canals and gondolas, it is certainly one of the most romantic cities in the world.

From our hotel, we were charmingly transported back and forth to the meeting on boats. Mignette and I were able to bring all 4 of our sons to that meeting and even our granddaughter Tristen (Jon and Brigid's daughter) as well. We were delighted by all parts of Venice, including St. Mark's Square, the Bridge of Sighs, and even the pigeons in the Piazza San Marco. At the conclusion of the IPTA meeting, we ended up taking a scenic trip by train to Rome, where the 18th TTS meeting was taking place.

The meeting in Rome was superb for many reasons, not the least of which was the opportunity for me to personally meet and talk to Pope John Paul II. At the 7th meeting, also in Rome, I had seen the crowning of Pope John Paul I (August 26, 1978) and had participated with the other officers of our society in a general audience with him shortly after his coronation. However, in 2000, Pope John Paul II had been asked by TTS to support the use of organs from living and deceased donors to help others in need. He agreed to our request and issued an encyclical in this regard. One of the reasons for our meeting with Pope John Paul II was to thank him for all he had done to encourage clinical organ transplants, nationally and internationally. For me, it was a thrill to meet him in person, to shake his hand, and to speak with him. Fortunately, my family was also there to soak in the experience as well. While waiting to meet the pope, my wife sat near famed singer Andrea Bocelli, who was also anxiously waiting for his individual audience with the pope. Later that evening, Bocelli performed a brilliant concert for TTS. He truly has one of the great operatic voices in the world.

My family and I toured all parts of Rome, including the Coliseum, St. Peter's Square, and Vatican City. The Sistine Chapel was in the process of being renovated at that time. Half of the old ceiling was clouded by the effects of smoke and time. It was instructive to compare it to the newly restored portions.

Boston, Moscow, St. Petersburg, Cyprus, Taiwan, Beijing, Athens, London, Madrid, Colorado Springs, Barcelona, Venice, Rome, Jerusalem—those are just a few of the many wondrous places that stand out for me as highlights of my long, far-reaching career.

I worked long and hard both before and during all of those trips, yet I was also blessed to be able to share so many sights and highlights with my family. The global field of transplantation has been a passport to indelible memories for me, even as out-of-this-world patient care always remained my continual mission.

Chapter Eighteen
FAMILY

This is a difficult chapter to write because it is so personal. Any detailed discussion of my family and the accomplishments of my children could appear as excessive as a Christmas card letter. However, I would be remiss if they were not included in this account of my life, given their vital role in my personal and professional well-being.

Of all the decisions one makes in life, probably the most important is picking the right spouse. If that decision is sound, then all of the others will be much easier and much more likely to be successful. As I already mentioned in Chapter Three, I was very fortunate to have found what I consider the perfect mate, Aryls Viola Mignette Anderson. Her third given name came from her mother, a Swedish emigrant, who named her daughter after the fragrant flower mignonette, which grew in her grandfather's hometown in Sweden. Perhaps fortunately, her mother misspelled it so that it became Mignette. My wife has always used Mignette as her first name. She is referred to by many of us as Mig or, occasionally, Migie or Midge. To my knowledge, I have never found another Mignette. However, our son Paul and his wife, Julie, named their first daughter Sophia Mignette; needless to say, Mignette was extremely pleased to have her granddaughter bear her name.

Mignette has all the attributes that any man would seek in a wife. First and foremost, she was and is beautiful inside and out. Brought up on a farm in western Minnesota and then trained as a nurse, she acquired an array of outstanding skills. She worked in the fields, performed endless chores, and to this day can fix almost anything mechanical or electrical. As the oldest of 6 children, she helped take care of her 5 siblings. She was raised with strict social and moral principles and with a strong religious faith, to top off all of her other laudable attributes. She truly is the moral rudder of our family.

With a wife like that, my personal life was bound to be successful. Mignette made it easy for me to get involved in my professional life, since I knew everything at home was in good hands. We were and are the best of friends, as well as devoted companions for nearly 60 years. She has been my teacher in many ways; she has done everything in her power to try to make me a better human being. However, I must admit that this is an ongoing, never-ending process, involving everything from minor social deficiencies like table manners to more weighty issues of public decorum.

Mignette had concerns about whether or not I treated my students, residents, and transplant fellows as thoughtfully as I should, primarily when she overheard my criticism of them over the phone or heard of charged interactions with them at the hospital. But I was always careful to point out that I never upbraided them in public, but rather waited for an opportunity to have a private conversation regarding any actions that concerned me as their mentor, particularly with regard to the treatment of patients, nurses, or other hospital personnel. The only time that I broke this rule was when we were in the operating room and a resident or fellow was ill-prepared for the procedure or made an inappropriate surgical decision: then and only then, I never hesitated to reprimand him or her on the spot, because surgical misadventures can never be tolerated under any circumstances. As surgeons, we have the health and even the life of a patient in our hands, and must always be at our best when performing operations. At times, my criticism of some students, residents, and fellows appeared too severe to Mignette, but having been a nurse she understood the importance of total preparation and the need for all surgeons to make optimal decisions.

As mentioned in earlier chapters, in our initial years as a married couple, I had the privilege of working with my wife when she was a nurse at the Lovelace Clinic in Albuquerque, where I was in the Air Force as a division surgeon for the 34th Air Division. When I was not busy at the air base or at the various aircraft control and warning sites that I serviced, I spent time at the Lovelace Clinic. I had the opportunity to work in the surgical suite of Bataan Memorial Hospital with Mignette and found her to be, along with her many other traits, a very able technical surgeon. After I was discharged from the service, during my surgical residency, she became pregnant with our oldest son, Jon, born in 1957 at the University of California, San Francisco (UCSF), hospital.

From that point on and to her credit, she gave up nursing and became a stay-at-home mom, raising 4 boys. In no way could I be more proud of them. However, I give all of the credit to her. In their early years, I found that I rarely got to know them because of my busy schedule as a resident and my time away traveling to research meetings. On my average day, I would leave in the morning before they were awake and return home after they were asleep. During some of my laboratory and postgraduate research years, I at least had time on the weekends to spend with our children, especially in Pittsburgh and La Jolla. But weekend downtime was particularly rare at the end of my surgical residency and at the beginning of my career at UCSF as an ambitious, very engrossed assistant professor of surgery.

In the mid-1960s, as vice chairman of the UCSF surgery department and director of its surgical research laboratories, I was deeply immersed in the development of the surgical research program and the transplant program, with myriad operative, laboratory, and administrative duties. In 1967, when I accepted the position as chairman of the Department of Surgery at the University of Minnesota, I made a vow: "never on Sunday." This meant that every Sunday would be a family day. Mignette and I would go nowhere without the children; they would have no one over to the house, nor would they go out and play with their friends on that day. Sundays involved going to church and then spending time at football games or at other sporting events, or just being together as a family. This gave me a regular opportunity to get to know my kids much better. Inevitably, though Sundays were sacrosanct, there were a few now and then when I had to leave for a medical or surgical meeting or for a patient emergency beyond the capability of my on-call or on-duty resident or fellow. But for the most part, the "never on Sunday" rule ensured plenty of reliable, beneficial interaction for us as a family.

Our oldest son, Jon, has always been very special, as is any firstborn child in any family. Mignette spent countless hours with him as a baby. She would read nursery rhymes to him (as she did to all the others). She states that when Jon was 2 years old, he had memorized several hundred nursery rhymes. She also read, to all 4 boys, stories from the encyclopedia, the Bible, and a variety of educational books. Their favorite was *Moby Dick*. In addition, she would have them sing everything that they needed to memorize, such as our address and telephone number.

Jon's first name is spelled without an "h" so that he would never be a junior; his second name, Arthur, was for Mignette's father, Arthur T.L. Anderson. Jon was a very gifted individual and a standout athlete at his high school in football and in track. All of our sons went to public school and graduated from Minneapolis Central High School, located in the center of south Minneapolis. The students were predominantly African American, which helped make school a wonderful experience for Jon and his brothers. They all grew up colorblind. Their school years helped prevent the development of any prejudice toward any race.

While our boys were playing football at Minneapolis Central High, I would make every effort to get all my work done so that I could attend as many Friday afternoon football games as possible. During the summer, we spent time at our summer home in Wisconsin on the St. Croix River, enjoying water sports; I also loved gardening. As a result of my weekend outdoor exposure and my Armenian heritage, my complexion turned quite dark every summer. One early autumn Friday, I was sitting with Mignette in the stands watching the football game. One of our sons' black teammates said to Jon and David, "I see that your father is married to a white woman." They just laughed and said "you're absolutely right."

Jon was a talented artist and still is. He decided that he wanted to be an architect and enrolled at Gustavus Adolphus College in nearby St. Peter, Minnesota, where Mignette had been a pre-nursing student. During his college years, Jon had 2 art shows featuring paintings he had completed in class. The primary courses that he took at Gustavus were in art and design, in preparation for admission to the architectural school at the University of Minnesota. However, after graduation, he became a free-agent acquisition for the Chicago Bears of the National Football League (NFL) as a middle linebacker—this was too much of a temptation to pass up. He accepted the offer to be an invited walk-on player. Although he played only in the preseason, he eventually lost his position to Michael Singletary.

Because it was too late to enter the architectural school at the University of Minnesota, Jon went to work for the Chicago Board Options Exchange (CBOE) as a "gopher." He enjoyed working there so much that he took the examination to be a trader and passed. He decided to give up his ambition to be an architect and stayed on at the Exchange as a stock trader, competing with all the Ivy League MBAs [Master of Buisness Administration holders]. With his friendly demeanor, Jon soon became very successful and was advised to start his own trading firm. Continuing success as a trader led to ownership of the largest privately owned firm on the CBOE and, eventually, employment of 55 traders. He subsequently sold that company, Mercury Trading. Along with our youngest son, Peter, he began a proprietary trading firm in the penthouse of a building across the street from the Board of Trade and the CBOE. Jon and Peter converted that proprietary trading firm to Option Monster, a securities and option brokerage firm as well as a media holding company. Option Monster is growing rapidly and currently has over 300 employees.

In order to advertise Option Monster, Jon and Peter began appearing periodically on a national TV program called "Fast Money" on CNBC. Their appearances increased the program's viewership numbers so much that the moderator, Dylan Rattigan, asked Peter to become a regular. Peter accepted the offer and now appears 5 nights a week on this program, which airs live at 4:00 p.m. (with a repeat showing at 7:00 p.m. Central Standard Time). He explains current market trends and offers financial advice. Jon still runs Option Monster as well as their private financial corporation, where he works as a financial analyst and appears as a frequent guest expert on "Fast Money." In addition, Jon travels nationally and internationally, giving invited lectures on financial analysis and on how to understand stock options. He and his wife, Brigid, have 2 children.

Our second son, David, was born in 1959, while I was a senior resident at UCSF. David also went to Gustavus Adolphus College, where he was a pre-med major. He was my first hope to follow in my footsteps in surgery and did extremely well in college, with an almost perfect grade point average. But unfortunately, his dyslexia required him to work night and day and frequently on weekends, going over and over all his class subjects, in order to achieve those top grades. David was also an outstanding football player as well as a track star, competing in the discus event. As a football standout, he played as an outside linebacker. In his senior year, he was co-captain with Jon of the Gustavus football team. Sadly, during the very last quarter of the last game that he played at Gustavus, David sustained a knee injury, resulting in the loss of both cruciate ligaments along with his medial collateral ligament. This injury was successfully repaired and he was invited to be a walk-on for the Green Bay Packers, who were very interested in this 6'4" 250-pound outside linebacker. However, after his physical examination, the Packers staff felt that, even though David's knee had healed, the risk of signing him (given the possibility of a subsequent injury to that knee) was greater than they wanted to assume.

David returned home to Minneapolis and was admitted to medical school at the University of Minnesota. He completed the first 2 years, but because of the constant studying mandated by his dyslexia, dropped out after his second year. He and our third son, Paul, became young entrepreneurs in the fast food business (bringing Popeye's Chicken to the Twin Cities). David has 5 children; he and his wife, Kris, home-schooled all of them. Their kids turned out to be excellent students. I must admit that I was against home-schooling, since all of our children had done so well in the bustle of the public schools, but I became a believer. Each year, all 5 of these grandchildren would take the Iowa standardized tests and would achieve a level at least 2 to 3 years ahead of their own chronological age. Our oldest granddaughter, Jessica, now 21, is a pre-med student and may be the doctor I've been waiting for. She is also an outstanding swimmer and concert pianist.

Our third son, Paul, was born in 1961 at Sharp Hospital in San Diego on Mignette's birthday, while I was a research fellow at the Scripps Clinic and Research Foundation in La Jolla. Paul went to my alma mater, the University of California, Berkeley, where he played football and was a standout linebacker. He was on the team when, with only 4 seconds left, they scored on Stanford to win the "Big Game" on November 20, 1982—with a series of rugby-type lateral passes that led to the most fantastic finish of any college football game ever played. It will always be remembered by sports announcers and other football fans as "THE PLAY."

Paul's major at Berkeley was theater arts. After graduation, he continued to do very well in football and briefly played for the Vancouver Lions of the Canadian Football League. Eventually, he ended up in Hollywood as a young aspiring actor. Although he was in 1 or 2 movies, he became disillusioned with the Hollywood scene and returned to Minnesota (where, as already mentioned, he joined David in the fast food business). Interestingly, Paul has also persisted with his acting career, landing some roles in local theaters in Minneapolis. He has also appeared in print and TV advertisements. He and his wife, Julie, have 3 children.

Our fourth son, Peter, was born in 1963 at the UCSF hospital, on my birthday (just as Paul had been born on his mother's birthday). As the youngest son with 3 older brothers, he had to fight for his very existence. That is probably why he became the best athlete of all 4 boys. In high school, he was an All-State football, basketball, and track and field star. He eventually went to the University of Minnesota, where he played football for 4 years and made the All Big Ten ranking. In addition, he was an Academic All-American and was voted the most valuable defensive player for 3 years by his teammates. (Eventually, he was even inducted into the Minnesota Sports Hall of Fame.) After college, Peter went on to play in the NFL with the Seattle Seahawks, the Minnesota Vikings, and the Tampa Bay Buccaneers. He finally finished up in Sacramento (in the World League of American Football), which had teams in

Barcelona, Frankfurt, London, and Montreal, as well as 6 in the United States. His team, the Sacramento Surge, won the final championship game in the World Bowl in Montreal. Having achieved a Bowl ring, he still had 2 knees that were functional, so he decided to quit.

Since he was also pre-med, Peter considered the possibility of going to medical school. However, he had been away from academics for 6 years. I told him it would be very difficult for him to catch up with his peers after such a long absence and suggested he should perhaps at least consider the possibility of working with Jon in Chicago at the CBOE. Peter decided to do so. He found he enjoyed working at the Exchange and became a "pit boss" for Jon's company, Mercury Trading. Eventually, when Jon sold the company, Peter went on to work with him as co-founder of their current business, Option Monster. As mentioned before, Peter is now on national television each night on "Fast Money." He's doing a first-class job. He and his wife, Lisa, have 2 children.

In discussing this chapter with Mignette, she wanted me to be sure to stress the fact that all 4 of our boys are quite devout in their religion. Jon and his Irish Catholic wife are raising their 2 absolutely beautiful daughters in the Catholic church. The other 3 boys attend various Protestant churches, and as Mignette pointed out, are avid readers of the Bible. This part of their moral fiber is certainly, once again, directly a result of their mother's example and influence.

All in all, I couldn't be more proud of our 4 boys and what they've accomplished and will continue to accomplish. I am immensely grateful as well for the 12 grandchildren that they've given us. Since Mignette frequently babysits Paul's kids, I've had a chance to see our grandchildren growing up and experience what I missed when my own children were little. It's been a wonderful life for all of us. Even though Mignette as a young nurse had gone to postwar California with the idea of having new adventures, there and around the globe, she ended up married to a native Californian, returning with him to Minnesota without uttering a word of disappointment. She was totally supportive of our move back to her beloved home state and has made Minnesota an ideal home base for all of us.

Chapter Nineteen
THE BEST OF TIMES,
THE WORST OF TIMES

As I look back now on what occurred with the development of Minnesota antilymphocyte globulin (MALG, often shortened to ALG), I keep thinking of Charles Dickens' opening words from *A Tale of Two Cities*: "It was the best of times, it was the worst of times, it was the age of wisdom, it was the age of foolishness...."

THE BEST OF TIMES...

The beginning of the ALG saga dates back to the early 1960s, when the first successful nontwin kidney transplants were being reported. In our program at the University of California, San Francisco (UCSF), as in the other 5 or 6 programs performing clinical kidney transplants at that time, it became apparent that we now had an alternative therapy for patients dying with end-stage renal disease, besides chronic hemodialysis.

THE WORST OF TIMES...

But as kidney transplant programs progressed, the results with deceased donor kidneys were very poor: the average kidney graft survival rate at 1 year posttransplant was less than 40%; at 5 years, less than 25%. At UCSF, we primarily performed living related donor kidney transplants, which could achieve a 60% graft survival rate at 5 years. Our only immunosuppressive drugs in those days were azathioprine (Imuran) and prednisone, so we were looking for another agent that could improve survival statistics (both for living donor and for deceased donor transplants). We needed more opportunities for individuals who were dying of kidney failure to be treated successfully. I felt that ALG might be the ticket.

My active interest in ALG was stimulated in 1963 by reading an article in the journal *Nature* (33) about the effectiveness of antilymphocyte serum in promoting the survival of skin grafts in rats, as reported by Sir Michael Woodruff of Scotland. I already knew Woodruff. In 1960, I had applied for a fellowship in his laboratory, but was told that I would have to wait 1 year. That was why I instead went to work with Dr. Frank Dixon, training in immunopathology research in Pittsburgh. At several transplant meetings, I had discussed with Woodruff how he prepared his antilymphocyte serum; we continued to enjoy active correspondence afterward. In 1965, fellow transplant surgeon Dr. Tony Monaco and I talked about his own studies on the use of antilymphocyte serum in mice. I rapidly realized that it would be an excellent immunosuppressive agent for organ transplant recipients.

Dr. Thomas Starzl in Colorado also recognized the potential that ALG had as a very effective immunosuppressive agent for transplants. His program began in 1964; the horse was selected as the serum donor for their ALG. Dr. Yoji Iwasakai, a Japanese surgeon, led the Colorado team in developing the process of manufacturing ALG, which they tested in dogs undergoing experimental kidney and liver transplants. In 1966, the first human patients in the world were treated with ALG at the Colorado General and the Denver Veterans Affairs (VA) hospitals. I visited Colorado and observed that human kidney allograft rejection was partially avoided during ALG treatment and that, in addition, ALG was also used effectively to reverse established rejection (34).

THE WORST OF TIMES...

However, because of the relatively crude preparation that was then in use, the ALG serum had to be injected intramuscularly into the patient's buttocks. The pain was so extreme that most transplant recipients in Colorado began to refuse ALG treatment. In addition, recipients' own immune systems began to react to and manufacture antibodies to the ALG, frequently rendering it useless after the initial treatment period.

THE BEST OF TIMES...

As stated in Chapter Eight, when I came back to California from Colorado, I asked Dr. Robert Perper, my first Ph.D. student, to see if he could sufficiently purify ALG so that it could be safely given intravenously. Perper accomplished this feat (16). We began using ALG intravenously, along with Imuran and prednisone, for our kidney transplant recipients at UCSF.

At first, we obtained the lymphocytes and thymocytes (lymphoid cells) to inject into horses to make ALG from patients who had undergone cardiac surgery. But the numbers of lymphoid cells per patient that were available for injection per horse varied continually. As a result, the potency of our ALG was inconsistent. So, as detailed in Chapter Eleven, we began exploring the possibility of obtaining a much more consistent source of lymphoid cells to inject into horses. In 1967, when I left UCSF to go to Minnesota, I brought with me the method that Perper had developed for purifying horse antilymphocyte globulin. The crucial remaining step was to find a consistent source of lymphoid cells for injection into horses.

I was aware of the work being done by Dr. George Moore of Roswell Park Hospital in Buffalo, New York. I went there and was intrigued by the way its researchers were growing large quantities of lymphocytes in culture. Moore sent his own cells, grown in culture 2 or 3 times, for us to use in injecting our horses in Minnesota. After returning home, I handed the project over to Dr. Allen Moberg, a surgical fellow in our department. Using the techniques developed by Moore at Roswell Park, Moberg began growing lymphocytes. We now had our own lymphocyte colony; when grown in culture, these lymphocytes transformed into immature precursor lymphoblasts, which contained the identity of both T and B lymphocytes. Our antilymphoblast serum would now be able to destroy transplant recipients' antibody-containing B cells as well as T lymphocytes, which are responsible for cellular immunity.

The next step was to find a reliable source of available and healthy horses. I contacted the veterinary school at the University of Minnesota campus in nearby St. Paul. A group of horses over there was used primarily by veterinary students for teaching gynecologic and obstetrical anatomy. We agreed to pay the students (who welcomed this educational project as well as the extra income) to inject the horses with cultured lymphocytes and withdraw blood; separate the plasma; and return the red blood cells to the horses. The resulting plasma was used to make a new form of ALG, specifically labeled MALG.

In 1968, we began using the investigational drug ALG clinically for our transplant recipients. We also conducted a series of experiments to examine the efficacy of ALG for nontransplant patients with multiple sclerosis, who volunteered and who gave informed consent. Multiple sclerosis possibly represents a variant of an autoimmune disease, so the patients who signed up for our study hoped that their condition might improve with the use of ALG. We exchanged skin grafts between these multiple sclerosis study participants, and found that ALG could increase skin graft survival by as many as 7 days. Of all organ grafts, skin grafts are the most difficult to survive rejection. Our skin graft study results indicated not only that we could give ALG safely and painlessly, but also that it was a very effective immunosuppressive agent.

In 1969, we published an article describing the clinical use of ALG. Coauthors included Moore, who had taught us how to grow lymphocytes; Dr. Robert Good, the University of Minnesota bone marrow transplant pioneer who was our consultant in this program; and Dr. J. Bradley Aust, a transplant surgeon on our faculty before my arrival as department chairman. In that article (35), we reported on 18 of our kidney recipients who received ALG and 11 who did not. The ALG group had 0.7 rejection episodes per patient; the non-ALG group had twice as many, 1.4 per patient. None of the ALG group developed antibodies against ALG. Our experience allayed the concern, which had been expressed by the Colorado transplant surgeons, that recipients would react to injected ALG. In actuality, when given intravenously, our purified ALG resulted in the development of tolerance to the ALG by the host (i.e., by the transplant recipient). This meant that ALG could be given repeatedly, without fearing an antibody reaction in subsequent injections.

In April 1969, I presented a paper in Cincinnati, Ohio, to
the American Surgical Association on the preparation and
purification of ALG and on its immunosuppressive properties in
humans, a paper that was later published in the *Annals of Surgery*
(36). In October 1969, Dr. Henry Gewerz presented a paper in San
Francisco to the American College of Surgeons that described the
induction of immunologic tolerance to ALG in humans (37). As was
well-known to immunologists, a highly purified protein given
intravenously can frequently result in tolerance to the antigen by
the host.

On December 9, 1970, I submitted to the U.S. Food and
Drug Administration (FDA) an investigational new drug (IND)
application for equine ALG. In addition, we requested cost recovery
for the manufacture of this product. The FDA accepted our request.
The IND application designated the University of Minnesota,
Department of Surgery as the sponsor, and I was the principal
investigator. In 1971, I realized that I could not spend the time
necessary to fully develop and administer ALG production, or to
prepare the mountains of required regulatory reports. Therefore, I
recruited Mr. Richard Condie, who I remembered as an outstanding
immunologist (part of Good's immunology group) who was at
Roosevelt Hospital in New York, to come to the University of
Minnesota. Condie served as director of our ALG program until
September 1992. The financial affairs of the ALG program, as well
as those of our Department of Surgery, were managed by our senior
administrator, Mr. James Coggins.

Thanks to our publications and through word of mouth,
other transplant surgeons—many of whom questioned whether we
were getting the results we were reporting—would come to the
University of Minnesota and review our books and patient histories.
They found that in fact, we were achieving a 15% to 20%
improvement in our kidney graft and patient survival rates in
recipients on ALG. More and more, transplant surgeons started to
request our ALG for their own programs. However, we could not
give it to them because of FDA regulations. We therefore requested
FDA approval to supply ALG to other transplant programs and to

receive cost recovery from transplant programs requesting ALG. The FDA approved cost recovery based on our expenses with respect to the use of horses, the preparation of cultured cells, and the process of manufacturing and purifying ALG. We met with FDA officials at least every year, sometimes more frequently. They would come to Minnesota and check our books. They examined our results, as well as the results of other transplant units using ALG.

Eventually, the FDA told us that, in order to receive approval of our ALG for clinical use, it would have to be manufactured in a facility that was specifically licensed by the FDA. So, we hired an architect who had worked for the FDA to design such a facility, to be built on our St. Paul campus.

By 1976, we reported on our 7-year experience with ALG for deceased donor kidney recipients, once again presenting a paper at the American Surgical Association meeting and then publishing it in the *Annals of Surgery* (38). In that article, we described 587 kidney recipients who received ALG: at 2 years posttransplant, our patient survival rate was 76%; graft survival, 63%. At 5 years posttransplant, our patient survival rate was 64%; graft survival, 42%. At 1 year posttransplant, our graft survival rate in 184 consecutive deceased donor kidney recipients was 75%, as compared with only 40% in 1967.

During the 22 years in which ALG was used, staff members of the FDA continued to come to Minnesota to examine our books and results. From time to time, they would make suggestions to Condie of better ways to follow FDA regulations. Of note, every new advance we made in the developing field of clinical organ transplantation was documented and published in the medical literature, both in the United States and abroad.

Given our now widely published results on the effectiveness of ALG when tested against standard therapy, the use of ALG soon became accepted as standard therapy in a variety of transplant centers throughout the United States. In 1982, a Canadian cyclosporine study group under the leadership of Dr. P.F. Halloran (39) reported on 19 patients randomized to "standard therapy" using prophylactic ALG (as well as Imuran and prednisone) vs. 26 patients randomized to a new drug, cyclosporine (as well as Imuran and prednisone). Discussion of their results indicated that ALG was as effective as cyclosporine, when used as an adjunct to Imuran and prednisone. In addition, Halloran's group stated that there was some evidence ALG may even be superior to cyclosporine. In 1988, in the journal *Transplantation* (40), Halloran's group authored a multivariate analysis of 200 consecutive deceased donor kidney transplants, once again showing the safety of ALG, whether recipients had early graft function, delayed graft function, or diabetes.

Because of the increasing evidence of ALG's efficacy, we continued to supply it to a large number of transplant units. Given the improved results with ALG, thousands of lives were saved. And so it was out of medical need that we continued to supply ALG to major transplant programs, whether they could pay or not, until we could receive a full license from the FDA. Our only holdup was building our FDA-licensed facility, because we had to wait until we had accumulated enough financial reserves from ALG production. When the facility was completed on the St. Paul campus, we applied to the FDA for a product license in 1989 and for a facility license in 1992.

THE WORST OF TIMES…

I believe we were only about 3 to 4 months away from receiving full approval from the FDA for manufacturing ALG when 2 of the pharmaceutical houses that had competing products found that very few transplant programs were using their form of ALG. Their drug representatives tried to sell their ALG to transplant programs throughout America, but were frequently denied. Instead, everyone was quite pleased with the consistency and the efficacy of our ALG. Consequently, those 2 pharmaceutical houses complained to the FDA that we were unfair competition. I soon became aware that the FDA was greatly influenced by the pharmaceutical houses. At the insistence of 1 particular pharmaceutical house, the FDA looked for ways to stop the licensure of our ALG. In the summer of 1992, a transplant program in San Diego discovered a leak in a bottle of our ALG. The FDA used that report as a reason to put ALG on clinical hold until the problem could be corrected. From that point on, even though we fixed the problem that led to that leaky vial, we were never allowed to use ALG again.

In addition, the FDA and the National Institutes of Health (NIH) enjoined the University of Minnesota from illegally "selling" ALG, **something we never did!** Moreover, when our ALG program was investigated, it was found that the major uses of ALG reserve funds were all laudatory and legitimate. For instance, in addition to constructing the ALG building, the funds were used for transplant faculty and support staff salaries; laboratory, equipment, and office expenses; and outpatient services for transplant patients.

It should be noted that by 1992, more than 60,000 patients had been treated with ALG. As previously mentioned, the randomized double-blind trial in Canada had clearly demonstrated the efficacy and safety of our ALG. Participating centers had been reporting kidney transplant results that were at least 15% better than those achieved without ALG. In 1992 alone, we produced 75,000 grams of ALG. It was used by more than 160 transplant units. When our ALG program went on trial in 1995, a very careful search by the Federal Bureau of Investigation (FBI) was described of all of the units that used it. After a 2½-year investigation, the FBI came up with only 9 deaths out of 60,000 patients who had used ALG; only 2 of those 9 deaths could be directly attributed to ALG. In both those cases, ALG had been given inappropriately. Therefore, ALG's safety record was even better than that of aspirin.

Looking back, I don't know what I could have done differently, as the chairman of the surgery department of a public university medical school that focused on research, education, and patient care. We were not and are not a private, for-profit pharmaceutical house with deep pockets and legions of lawyers. Although I was the principal investigator on our IND application, regulatory matters fell to Condie as director of our ALG program. He would report to me on a weekly, and sometimes on a twice-weekly, basis regarding what was going on in the ALG program. I would try to help him in any way I could so that the program continued to be successful. However, as chairman of the Department of Surgery, I was also responsible for the training of more than 100 surgical residents and 200 medical students who rotated through our wards and clinics. Many laboratories and research activities throughout the department were under my jurisdiction as well. Our very active transplant program required countless hours in the operating room as well as countless hours training transplant fellows.

I would now and then hear directly from the FDA about, say, an overdue report or a specific information request. I always passed such items along to Condie and I was usually advised that they had been taken care of. In the 22 years that the FDA oversaw our ALG program, it was never put on clinical hold until, as mentioned, 1992. But in the decades before that, the FDA had always indicated to me that any problems were being solved or were not of a nature that required further action. Thus, in 1992 when we were put on clinical hold, I was extremely surprised that we had not been warned. I was also surprised that we had not been given a chance to meet whatever requirements the FDA felt were necessary.

I was even more surprised by the NIH assertion that its officials did not know we were in the business of manufacturing ALG. My extensive time serving on NIH study sections and the many reports that I had received indicated that the NIH had considered our ALG the gold standard for immunosuppressive antibodies. Everything that we had accomplished was always presented at surgical meetings or transplant meetings, here and abroad. At no time was anyone in the dark. The FDA made frequent visits to Minneapolis. On several occasions, we went to Washington to discuss our ALG program at the request of FDA administrators. I'm sure that the paperwork should have been done better, but our ALG manufacturing program had started out as an academic operation, based on our scholarly and clinical work on behalf of our own patients. Similar programs for making ALG were ongoing in several academic transplant programs. Then, because of our ALG's success, its use spread to more than 160 institutions by 1992.

I was especially surprised by the headline-grabbing theatrics of the FDA's method of disclosing its clinical hold. On August 13,

1992, the deputy director of the FDA Center of Biological Evaluation and Research traveled to Minneapolis personally to deliver a letter to the University of Minnesota's then-president, Nils Hasselmo, and to me as Department of Surgery chairman. This letter closed down our ALG program after 22 years of operation. During the ensuing 2½ years, our program was investigated by the FDA, the FBI, the Internal Revenue Service (IRS), 2 law firms representing the University of Minnesota, and the office of the U.S. Attorney for the District of Minnesota. The investigation focused on alleged FDA regulatory violations, including whether ALG had been illegally sold in interstate commerce, whether adverse reactions had been concealed, and whether appropriate patient consent had been obtained.

In addition, in an effort to find evidence of outward personal gain, the IRS was brought in to look for diversions of ALG funds to my personal benefit. They found none.

I continued to be surprised by the snowball effect of the legal drama we were caught in. In April 1995, criminal charges were filed against me in U.S. District Court in St. Paul. The major count of the indictment alleged a conspiracy to violate various provisions of the federal Food, Drug, and Cosmetic Act and the Public Health Service Act by "illegally" charging 79 million dollars for ALG during a 22-year period. I was astounded: after all, our ALG program had received authorization for cost recovery by the FDA way back in 1970. And per our IND application, cost recovery had been officially granted, implicitly and explicitly, in 1989. I was also charged with failing to report adverse reactions (for example, those 9 deaths) and with failing to obtain informed consent from patients. This alleged conspiracy, according to the indictment, was to enhance my "personal power and prestige" through financial gain and otherwise.

THE BEST OF TIMES...

As soon as the criminal charges were filed, many individuals—family, friends, and patients—stepped forward to ask how they could help. I was immensely grateful for all of the help, but in particular for the instrumental efforts of my wife, Mignette, and 3 of her sisters and 1 brother. They diligently went over 2 million pieces of paper that were part of the discovery phase for my upcoming trial. They spent 12 to 18 hours a day, 7 days a week, collating and organizing all of the paperwork, using our living room as their base office. They copied documents from the Minneapolis Courthouse as well. This was a labor of love that I can never fully repay. The indispensable work they did made it easy for my lawyers to find the necessary documents for my defense.

In addition, one of my former transplant fellows, Dr. Caliann Lum, spent those 9 pre-trial months going through the interminable records of the 9 hospitals involved in the 9 deaths that allegedly might have been due to ALG. She stepped down from working as a transplant surgeon just to accomplish this research. Her firsthand expertise was, of course, one of the reasons that we had all of the medically accurate information on these 9 patients, enabling us to prove that, most likely, none of those deaths were directly due to ALG. In fact, 2 of those deaths were definitely due to inappropriate administration of ALG, despite adequate labeling in product brochures that clearly stated the method of administration. Lum was also assisted by a family friend in this effort. There were many others—too many to mention—who I knew were also compiling information and helping my lawyers thoroughly prepare. I am eternally thankful.

THE WORST OF TIMES…

I was not accused of personally receiving any ALG money, yet I was charged with embezzlement related to travel expenses, mail fraud, tax fraud, and obstruction of justice. These charges were described by the lawyers as "piling on."

The trial began on January 16, 1996, before U.S. District Court Judge Richard H. Kyle in St. Paul. The first charge was that we had "illegally" charged transplant centers for ALG. But during the trial, the evidence established that the FDA did not object to our cost recovery proposal set forth in our IND application and was aware that we distributed and charged for ALG for 22 years. The initial charge in 1971 for cost recovery was $55 per gram, with 5 increases to $235 per gram by 1988. The FDA expressly approved our charging in 1989, albeit at $134 per gram rather than our previous $235 per gram. The FDA's practice of allowing cost recovery during the 1970s was pursuant to an unwritten policy confirmed in a 1973 opinion from the FDA's own general counsel.

The second charge was that we had failed to report adverse reactions in patients receiving ALG. It must be understood: these patients awaiting a transplant had multiple medical problems that frequently clouded diagnosis of any complications posttransplant. Physicians testified at the trial that patients were frequently fluid-overloaded after surgery, a condition that would cause respiratory difficulties with ALG. Of the total of 9 patients who died, allegedly because of ALG, 2 were University of Minnesota patients, including a 35-year-old man with diabetes who underwent a pancreas transplant. Although I was not involved in his case, I was a coauthor of the paper reporting his fatal anaphylactic reaction presented at the annual American Surgical Association meeting in Toronto, Ontario, in April 1984 (41). The other Minnesota patient died of multiple sclerosis and cardiac arrest, according to his death certificate. I was not involved in his care either and was unaware of the circumstances of his death. Of the 7 other patient deaths at other transplant centers, only 2 had been brought to my attention at the time of their deaths. In both cases, ALG was administered inappropriately, without following the instructions for administration that were part of our product information. Thus, no one made any effort to hide deaths or adverse reactions. To the contrary, all of the adverse reactions our program had seen were published in scientific articles or presented at transplant and surgical meetings by the Minnesota group.

The third charge was that we had failed to obtain informed consent from ALG patients. Yet a consent form, specifically for ALG, was drafted in 1975 and used for about 10 years. By 1985, however, the form was no longer used, for reasons that remain unclear; perhaps it was simply a matter of institutional memory, since ALG had long become our standard therapy. University of Minnesota employees stated during the trial that, after the transplant unit moved into the new hospital, the forms were not around, presumably having been misplaced. I thought the forms were used, to the best of my knowledge, right up through 1992, and was surprised to learn that this was not the case. But even so, all transplant patients at the University of Minnesota were routinely provided with detailed information about the entire transplant process and the drugs that they would be using, including ALG.

Virtually all of the patients interviewed in preparation for the trial confirmed that they believed they were knowledgeable about the drugs and that all of their questions had been thoroughly answered. Although some patients were unaware of ALG's investigational status, they invariably added that it made no difference to them as long as their physicians recommended using it. Testimony indicated that the education of patients at the University of Minnesota Transplant Center was among the best in the country.

THE BEST OF TIMES...

When the government rested its case on February 13, 1996, Kyle entered a judgment of acquittal in my favor on all FDA-related counts (deeming them baseless, not even worth the jury's time to consider). The only counts that remained were those added charges of embezzlement related to travel expenses, mail fraud, tax fraud, and obstruction of justice. A certified public accountant employed by my defense attorneys had pored over the books over a 2-year period but could find no evidence to support any of those added charges. As a result, on February 21, 1996, the jury returned a verdict of Not Guilty on all remaining counts.

I was quite relieved and returned to the operating room the following morning to perform a pediatric kidney transplant. To this day, I have continued with my surgical practice and my practice in transplantation, and will do so as long as I am able. Patient care has always been my highest priority and my first love.

THE WORST OF TIMES...

My biggest disappointment was the fact that the administration of the University that I had faithfully worked for throughout my entire 25 years as chairman of the Department of Surgery had decided to aid the prosecution, headed by the U.S. Attorney in Minnesota. The University administration spent millions of dollars in support of the prosecution. They hired the largest law firm in Minnesota, as well as attorneys from Washington, D.C., who came to Minneapolis at tremendous expense, in an effort to place the indictment solely on my shoulders. They sought to avoid any administrative culpability or responsibility. I would have hoped that they would have carefully reviewed the facts of the case before pointing a finger at a loyal member of the faculty who had received the University's highest honor, having been elected a Regents professor in 1985. Unfortunately, their decision not to at least take a neutral position in this saga sent a bad message to university professors throughout this country and abroad, who were justifiably concerned that a university administration would not at least attempt to support one of its own faculty members.

Finally, it was paradoxical and disconcerting that the FDA not only acquiesced in, but also encouraged, the widespread distribution of ALG across the country, thus enhancing its status as standard therapy, only to later file criminal charges against the principal investigator because the investigational drug was in fact used as standard therapy. The commentary of the presiding judge, I think, says it all: "Converting all of this, however, to be a criminal proceeding of the magnitude that we saw here, it seems to me, has gone or did go beyond the bounds of common sense. We had a program here in Minnesota, which for all of its problems and shortcomings was a good program, literally saved thousands of lives. It should have been run better and it wasn't, but I have serious doubts as to whether that type of program should have been subject to a criminal proceeding of this kind.

"The FDA, as I indicated, was certainly aware of what was going on, and yet they came in here...to testify that somehow they were hoodwinked by this defendant and his colleagues and the other people at the University"(42).

What happened with our ALG program remains a concern to clinical investigators throughout the United States, as well as abroad. The FDA chose to file felony-level criminal charges to address regulatory issues. Criminalizing an alleged failure to report possible adverse reactions to an investigational drug presents many problems. As just 1 example, transplant recipients are a complex patient population: they have many illnesses and are on many medications. Filing such overblown threatening charges is not, in my opinion, a proper route to regulatory compliance.

The 1 question I'll always think about is this: If we were not complying with all of the regulations despite being monitored by the FDA for 22 years, why were we not put on clinical hold beforehand? Incidentally, all of the transplant surgeons I have talked to since have said that if our ALG were available today, they would use it for their patients. Sadly, it would cost about 15 to 20 million dollars and 3 to 4 years of costly and complicated clinical trials to obtain FDA licensure. Such massive financial, legal, and administrative hoops are obviously beyond the scope of any single academic transplant center, as I found out.

THE BEST OF TIMES...

But I am forever glad that our ALG extended the lives of more than 60,000 transplant recipients from the late 1960s through the early 1990s. Since 1992, survival results in transplant recipients have improved with newly discovered immunosuppressive agents. The need for an immunosuppressive antibody such as our ALG continues, in order to deliver complete treatment for transplant patients; I am pleased that our ALG led the way for the products and strategies that took its place. Despite all the foolishness of the FDA's negativistic regulatory overkill in our case, our ALG made a lasting difference in the lives of so many patients, caregivers, and transplant centers. And its demise has much to teach all of us still.

Chapter Twenty
THE CHAIR

On February 21, 1996, I was acquitted of all criminal charges brought against me by the federal government. Although the administration at the University had initiated the investigation and supported the prosecution, on February 22 I returned to the University to perform a kidney transplant in a small child. I enjoy all aspects of transplant surgery, but transplants in children are the most emotionally rewarding of all. My professional life at that point involved operative surgery at least 3 days a week. The rest of my time was spent teaching—during our classroom-style Grand Rounds, while making patient rounds, and in the operating room itself. In addition, as I had done throughout my entire career, I continued to write articles describing our continuing progress in the field of transplantation and general surgery. I continued to chronicle our Department of Surgery's research in the laboratory, and our clinical findings on the ward, as a testament to this evolving field. By contributing manuscripts to medical journals and presenting at symposia, I helped share our medical breakthroughs and challenges, nationally and internationally. I remain convinced that transplantation, the most important medical advance of the 20th century, will continue to evolve and thrive.

Having resigned as chairman of the Department of Surgery, I no longer had many of my previous administrative responsibilities. Still, I played an ongoing role in the administration of our transplant program, as I had done in the past. With a relative decrease in my overall administrative responsibilities, I now found more time to accept invitations to speak at surgical and transplant conferences. I was now also able to accept visiting professorships at the many institutions where former trainees were either the surgery department chair or the transplant program director.

Within a year or so after the trial, many members of the University administration had either left or been asked to leave for a variety of reasons. On the federal level, the director of the U.S. Food and Drug Administration (FDA) had left to become a dean at Yale University Medical School; eventually, he became a dean at my alma mater, the University of California, San Francisco (UCSF), but was recently discharged from that position over "financial problems." In Minneapolis and St. Paul, members of the U.S. attorney's office, including 1 who had sought to gain political office, also stepped back and, instead, are currently practicing law in several local firms.

Because of the trial, I paid a considerable sum of money (which I was hoping would serve for my retirement) as fees to my lawyers. Their 3-person law firm, Thompson, Lundquist & Sicoli, Ltd., put in nearly full-time effort for 3 years on the preparation and trial of my case. As is often the case, a segment of their costs went above the amount that they had originally agreed to charge. The 6-week trial conducted by Peter Thompson and John Lundquist was attended full-time by their 2 investigators, 2 clerks, and a documents specialist. Thompson and Lundquist attempted to obtain a contribution for these cost overruns from the University, but we were turned down.

After the criminal trial, the U.S. Department of Justice began prosecuting a whistleblower case, *Zissler v. Board of Regents, et al.,* against the University for a return of grant funds and penalties because of Minnesota antilymphocyte globulin (ALG) and other medical research programs. The Department of Justice asserted claims by the National Institutes of Health (NIH), the FDA, and others made by the whistleblower. This Department of Justice civil suit was directed at the University itself, whose central administration became quite concerned.

The University's assistant general counsel contacted Thompson and asked if he would allow me to answer questions by the Department of Justice lawyers to the effect that the ALG program had made a good effort to produce ALG according to the investigational new drug (IND) application, that we had faithfully worked with the FDA for 22 years concerning cost recovery, that we had attempted to follow regulatory rules as best we could, and that there was no effort to deceive the FDA or the NIH at any time.

Of course, this was the same position I had taken for the 4 previous years, but in a strange twist, the University now sought to align with my testimony!

Moreover, the University wanted to hire Thompson, my lawyer, to represent me at the deposition. For this cooperation, the University would pay his firm an amount of money that would equal well over half of the unpaid costs of the criminal trial. Thompson and Lundquist agreed, and I went through with the deposition.

Ultimately, this civil case was settled between the University and the federal government without a trial. The federal government grants to our own Department of Surgery were allowed to continue, among them the grant in organ transplantation, worth over a million dollars a year; at 40 years and counting, it is among the longest program project grants awarded by the NIH.

At the satisfactory conclusion of my deposition on November 20, 1998, Thompson sent a letter to Dr. Frank B. Cerra (then the senior vice president of health sciences), Dr. Alfred F. Michael (then dean of the Medical School), and Dr. David L. Dunn (at that time, professor and chairman of the Department of Surgery) regarding the establishment of a chair, in my name, in clinical transplantation. The exact contents of that letter are reproduced below:

Dear Dr.s Cerra, Dunn and Michael:

As you know, this week marked the end of the legal battles in the University's struggles with the Department of Justice. My client, and now dear friend, Dr. Najarian cooperated and our office assisted the University of Minnesota in Zissler v. Board of Regents, et al. This cooperation and the University's payment of fees in that civil matter has been gratifying as the first step toward what Dr. Najarian and I would hope would be a complete reconciliation of the University and Dr. Najarian.

His trials and tribulations with the F.D.A., IRS, FBI, U.S. Attorney's Office, and, yes, the University of Minnesota, have continued to leave him hurt and bewildered since 1993.

It is time the University take the next step in reconciling both privately and publicly with Dr. Najarian. I understand efforts have been underway during the past year to endow a John S. Najarian Chair in Transplantation. Such an action would be beneficial for the academics of the Medical School and the Department of Surgery, and would be a long overdue symbolic reconciliation with a man who gave 26 years of untiring and unparalleled service to the University. It would be a great relief to Dr. Najarian and his many friends, patients and supporters. This chair, of course, would be of great financial benefit to the University.

I have asked Mr. Vance Opperman to spearhead a fundraising effort to raise funds necessary to establish this chair.

I look forward to working with you gentlemen and the University to facilitate in any way I can this final chapter of the ALG affair. I am taking the liberty of informing a few of Dr. Najarian's colleagues and supporters of this initiative with a copy of this letter.

Very truly yours,
Peter Thompson

PT:tk

cc: John S. Najarian, M.D.
*   Vance Opperman, Esq.*
*   Dwight Opperman*
*   Stanley Hubbard*
*   Curt Carlson*
*   Richard Simmons, M.D.*
*   Arthur Matas, M.D.*

As seen above, one of the courtesy copies of Thompson's 1998 letter went to Stanley S. Hubbard, CEO of Hubbard Broadcasting. Two weeks after receiving the letter, Hubbard pledged

$50,000 toward a fund for a chair in my name. However, he stated that he would wait to give the money until the University progressed toward the goal of accepting an endowed chair in my name. In a meeting with Hubbard, as well as Steve Aanenson and Eric Aanenson (brothers active in the business community), Vance Opperman (another courtesy copy recipient and prominent member of my legal team) agreed to spearhead the fundraising effort. On January 6, 1999, Thompson gave the first donation toward the chair, $1,000. Six months later, Vance Opperman and his father, Dwight Opperman, each contributed $100,000. An anonymous gift of $24,000 arrived. Eric Aanenson gave another $25,000.

This money was collected by William A. Sullivan III, the executive vice president of the Institute for Basic and Applied Research in Surgery (IBARS), Edina, Minnesota. The money remained in IBARS from 2000 through 2005, at which time Dr. David A. Rothenberger became the interim chair of the Department of Surgery. Sullivan discussed with Rothenberger the possibility of starting an active campaign of general fundraising for the chair in surgery. Rothenberger contacted Hubbard, who eventually heard from University president Robert H. Bruininks, who saw no problem with a program to establish a chair in my name. University vice president Cerra gave Rothenberger the green light to begin the fund drive for the chair. Rothenberger continued with the effort even after a new permanent chairman of the Department of Surgery was appointed in 2006, Dr. Selwyn M. Vickers. The fundraising effort continued under Vickers.

Rothenberger enlisted the expertise of Erik J. Thurman, a fundraiser at the University of Iowa who began working for the Minnesota Medical Foundation (MMF) in our Department of Surgery in 2005. With the assistance of former transplant fellows Dr. Ronald M. Ferguson, Dr. David E.R. Sutherland, and Dr. Nancy L. Ascher, along with my former colleague Dr. Richard L. Simmons (another recipient of the 1998 letter), Thurman began sending letters to former residents and fellows, asking for contributions. By October 2007, the goal of $2 million had almost been reached when a final gift of $400,000 from Hubbard put the fund well over the top.

The funds for the endowed chair in my name came from more than 220 individual contributions, all greatly appreciated, from $50 on up. The fundraising campaign committee (Ascher, Ferguson, Simmons, Rothenberger, Sutherland, Vickers, and ex officio member Thurman) decided there should be a gala celebration. The celebration dinner was planned at the top of the 55-story IDS Tower downtown Minneapolis in a reception/banquet area called Windows on Minnesota. All the donors were formally invited to the celebration.

The celebration took place on Friday, November 30, 2007, sponsored by MMF with a major contribution from IBARS. The day began with a special celebratory luncheon at the University's Campus Club, with my wife, Mignette, and 3 of our sons and their wives in attendance. The luncheon included speeches from Becky Malkerson, MMF president and CEO; University vice president Cerra; and Dr. Deborah E. Powell, then dean of the Medical School. A closing speech was given by University president Bruininks, who officially presented me with the Endowed Scholars Medallion in honor of the John S. Najarian, M.D., Surgical Chair in Clinical Transplantation. On giving me the medallion, he stated that an endowed chair such as this was the highest honor that can be bestowed on a member of the University faculty.

That afternoon, in the major conference room of the Department of Surgery, a "Transplant Tribute" was held in my honor in the form of a 2-hour scientific symposium. The conference room rapidly filled to standing room only. The program, chaired by Vickers, featured talks by Simmons on the ALG program; Sutherland on the history of beta cell replacement strategies; Matas (a longtime colleague and recipient of the 1998 letter), via video, on our 40-year liaison with the NIH through our 1-of-a-kind program project grant; Ferguson on the evolution of immunosuppressive strategies at the University of Minnesota; and finally, Ascher on the importance of teamwork in transplantation. The symposium was excellent. I was given an opportunity to make comments after each of the speakers— quite an honor, considering that each has achieved so much in the field of transplantation after their training at our institution.

AFTERNOON SYMPOSIUM SPEAKERS

•*Selwyn M. Vickers, M.D.*
Jay Phillips Professor and Chair, Department of Surgery, University of Minnesota

• *Richard L. Simmons, M.D., Ph.D.*
Medical Director, University of Pittsburgh Health System; Medical Director and Chair, Institute for Quality and Medical Management; Vice Chair of Surgical Research, Department of Surgery, University of Pittsburgh

• *David E.R. Sutherland, M.D., Ph.D.*
Professor of Surgery; Head, Division of Transplantation; Director, Diabetes Institute for Immunology and Transplantation, University of Minnesota

• *Arthur J. Matas, M.D.*
Professor and Clinical Director, Kidney Transplant Program, Department of Surgery, University of Minnesota

• *Ronald M. Ferguson, M.D., Ph.D.*
Professor and Director, Division of Transplantation, Department of Surgery, Ohio State University

• *Nancy L. Ascher, M.D., Ph.D.*
Professor and Chair, Department of Surgery, University of California, San Francisco

Finally, the capstone was the celebratory dinner that evening at Windows on Minnesota in the IDS Tower. It was a beautiful affair attended by more than 250 guests. We were fortunate to have an absolutely clear night: the view of downtown Minneapolis and surrounding areas made for a remarkable backdrop, complete with an aerial view of our community's annual Holidazzle parade sponsored by Macy's North. Of the many touching speeches, one of the most important of all was from Hubbard. He is the true hero of this whole affair, having been involved from the beginning. He made sure that the chair in my name indeed came to pass. Over the 40 years that my family and I have enjoyed living in Minneapolis, he has been a dear friend and strong supporter. In addition to Hubbard, University vice president Cerra gave an outstanding and emotional presentation. Brad Madson, director of community relations for the Minnesota Vikings, presented me with an autographed football and jersey from the Associated Press NFL Offensive Rookie of the Year, Adrian Peterson. My longtime colleague, Barbara A. Elick, R.N., produced a wonderful 15-minute video featuring interviews with an array of faculty members and friends, including salutations from veteran newsman Tom Brokaw. Perhaps the most poignant part of the evening was "A Patient's Story" by Charles Fiske, now of Elmwood, Massachusetts, who updated the audience on his now-grown daughter Jamie, a quarter-century after her lifesaving liver transplant. Charlie Fiske is a most remarkable man; his presentation left many in tears and me with a lump in my throat.

Now the University has a chair in my name, which will go to the surgeon-scientist in charge of directing our transplant program. This chair, with its salary boost and, hopefully, with its name recognition appeal, will continue to attract outstanding transplant surgical scholars in perpetuity. For this I am most appreciative.

The chair will complement another substantive departmental honor, the John S. Najarian, M.D., Lecture in Transplantation, which began on May 15, 2007. The Najarian Lecture series was inaugurated with a mesmerizing appearance by Nobel laureate Dr. Joseph E. Murray. The 2nd Annual Najarian Lecture on May 6, 2008, brought France's legendary Dr. Jean-Michel Dubernard back to our campus to discuss his pioneering operations involving composite tissue grafts, including the first face transplant.

In particular, I am humbled and grateful that so many well-wishers gave so much of themselves for the chair and for every other milestone in my odyssey. The support that I have received from my family, friends, patients, residents, fellows, and coworkers made all

John S. Najarian M.D.

of this possible. The miracle of transplantation will remain alive and well as one of the jewels in the crown of the Department of Surgery, the Medical School, and the University of Minnesota.

Chapter 21
POSTSCRIPT

I didn't think I'd be writing this postscript. It came as quite a surprise, but has to be added to complete the story, even though after the first 20 chapters I had felt the book was finished. While putting the final touches on the preceding pages in the spring of 2008, I had been bothered with difficulty in seeing highway signs at night. I was examined by the chairman of ophthalmology at the University of Minnesota, who told me, as I suspected, that I had cataracts in both eyes. This is not an unusual diagnosis for an individual in his 80s, and I felt I should get this taken care of and did.

In preparation for the removal of my cataracts, I was required to undergo a physical examination, including electrocardiography. Unfortunately, like many doctors, I did not have a referring physician. So I asked one of my Department of Surgery's faculty members, Dr. Abhi Humar, to give me a physical examination and to act as my referring doctor. The electrocardiogram showed that I had what is called a left bundle branch block, which is a blockage of the electrical impulse from the heart's upper chamber to its lower pumping chamber. Such blockage is usually not a major problem; however, I went to a cardiologist for further evaluation.

The cardiologist felt that the blockage probably didn't mean much, but he did recommend a series of examinations including computed tomography (CT) angiography. As he explained, this is an excellent test, because clinicians can look at the vessels of the heart without actually having to inject any dye into the heart.

I wasn't very lucky when they tried to obtain the CT angiogram: there was too much calcium in my heart's vessels, so they couldn't get an adequate picture. Therefore, they set me up for direct cardiac angiography, in which a catheter is placed into the groin and travels up into the heart; dye is injected directly into the coronary vessels. In my case, this test showed that I had a major blockage of the anterior circumflex artery, which feeds the left anterior descending coronary artery and is often called the "widow maker." The blockage was in excess of 70%, meaning that it could completely block my artery at any moment. In many ways, I was quite lucky that this blockage was accidentally found, especially since I really did not have any symptoms of angina.

Subsequently, in May 2008, I underwent a quadruple coronary bypass, which involved connecting my left internal mammary artery to my left anterior descending artery. The cardiac surgeon (Dr. Tim Kroshus, one of my department's graduates) said he found a very large left internal mammary artery for connection to the left anterior descending artery. In addition, he and his team removed the saphenous vein from my left leg and divided it into 3 segments for the other 3 coronary artery connections. Thus, a quadruple coronary bypass was completed. The operation went very well.

I don't think the good Lord ever meant for anybody to split the breastbone and spread it open. This was the most painful part of my quadruple bypass. Healing of the breastbone alone requires at least 2 to 3 months.

I was only in the hospital for 5 days, although it seemed like an eternity. Their policy in the hospital was to check on the patient every hour during the day and every 2 hours during the night. Somebody would come into my room, awaken me, and ask how I was feeling, whether I was having pain, if I needed anything. This process was all right during the day, but at nighttime, when I was trying to sleep, it was another story. To have someone come in every 2 hours, turn on a bright light, and ask me questions was quite disruptive. All in all, my hospitalization made a better doctor of me, because I had an opportunity to see what our patients go through nowadays. I am now a much more sympathetic physician and surgeon than I already was. (It had been more than 6 decades since my previous hospitalization, back at age 12 for appendicitis.)

Fortunately, I was released from the hospital in 5 days. My wife, Mignette, a former surgical nurse, became my primary caregiver. She was superb. No one could ask for a better full-time nurse than Mignette. I'm sure her conscientious attentiveness was responsible for my rapid recovery.

Although I continued to get better, after about a month and a half, I once again began feeling short of breath. I thought this was just part of the healing process. Yet in addition, I was losing my appetite. I self-diagnosed that I had a tumor or other problem associated with my gastrointestinal tract, but also consulted the deputy chairman of the Department of Surgery, Dr. David Rothenberger, a colorectal surgeon. I asked him if he could determine why I was having all of these gastrointestinal problems. He ordered a variety of tests, including a double-contrast CT scan of my abdomen.

The CT scan revealed no tumor or gastrointestinal problem. Instead, it showed that my heart was surrounded by over 1,000 cc of fluid. My heart was pumping as best it could, albeit surrounded by this large amount of fluid. This condition has been described as Dressler's syndrome. Fortunately, it only occurs in about 3% to 5% of coronary bypass patients. The heart does not appreciate any invasion such as that performed in coronary bypass operations, yet in only 3% to 5% of such patients does the heart respond by making pericardial fluid. I was among them, for some reason: fluid had collected around my heart and compressed it, so that I could barely walk 10 yards without getting short of breath. Therefore, almost 2 months after my initial operation, I returned in July for more surgery. In that second major operation, the fluid was removed from around my heart, and a window was created between the pericardium and the pleural cavity. In that way, the fluid (which the heart could not dispose of on its own) could now go out into the pleural cavity, where it would be absorbed by the chest cavity. I was in the hospital for 3 days after this operation, but it set back my full recovery by another month or more.

I am now recuperating from this summer's startling surgical and procedural incursions. I am absolutely convinced that I was on the correct side of the knife for all of these years. I guess I was lucky that I had never needed to undergo any surgical procedure as an adult, until the year I turned 80.

I can now devote my time once again to teaching, writing, and lecturing. I look forward to more trips to see the 85-plus transplant fellows I've trained, who frequently invite me to their institutions as a visiting professor. I may no longer perform surgical procedures; I must admit that I do miss the operating room. Still, I'm so grateful to all of my students, fellows, and colleagues who sent cards, gifts of flowers and fruit, and, in particular, thoughts and prayers. To all of you, I give eternal thanks. I hope that I can continue to contribute in the field of medicine, my true professional love, for as long as I'm able.

Epilogue
THE FUTURE:
ANIMAL ORGANS?
STEM CELLS?

In looking to the future, we must be aware of the continuing differential between the individuals who are waiting for a transplant and the availability of grafts from human sources. At the present time, more than 100,000 individuals in the United States are waiting for a transplant; an estimated 10 to 15 of them die each day on the waiting list. In order to solve this problem, we are going to have to look at other sources of organs. The most obvious possibility is using animal organs.

With this in mind, I am struck by the fact that the most feasible animal source would be the pig—not only because of its size, but also because pig tissues have been safely used for many years. In addition to being a major source of food, pigs have been used for brain cell transplants in at least 11 people with Parkinson's disease, with no evidence of any transmission of pig viruses in any of those recipients. Pig heart valves have been placed in more than 1 million patients since 1950, once again, with no evidence of any transmission of pig viruses.

Pig skin has been clinically used to repair skin loss from burns. And pig intestinal tissue has been used to help repair damaged skin, cartilage, and bones since the 1990s.

Pig insulin has been used to regulate blood glucose in diabetic patients since the 1920s. Millions of people have received daily injections of pig insulin, in only partially purified form, with no evidence of any transmission of pig viruses or other microorganisms.

Finally, pig islets were transplanted into 14 patients in Sweden in the early 1990s. Evidence showed that some of the transplanted pig cells persisted in those recipients for several years, but once again, with no evidence of any transmission of pig viruses or other microorganisms.

Therefore, the pig has really been shown to be an excellent and quite safe source of organs. At the University of Minnesota, Dr. Bernhard Hering and his colleagues found that islets transplanted between different species (xenotransplants) do not trigger a fierce immune system attack (called hyperacute rejection). Rather, islet transplant recipients' immune response primarily resembles the rejection process between members of the same species. This finding suggests that islet xenotransplants do not carry the hyperacute rejection risk of some solid-organ xenotransplants; thus, rejection of pig islets could be prevented with the right mix of currently used immunosuppressive drugs.

Hering and his colleagues used cultured islets from pigs and transplanted them into diabetic Old World monkeys (rhesus and cynomolgus macaques). Some of the monkeys were made diabetic by the use of drugs (i.e., streptozotocin); others, by total surgical removal of their pancreas. The transplanted islets restored blood glucose control for more than 100 days. A similar experience was reported by Dr. Christian Larsen at Emory University in Atlanta; he transplanted islets from neonatal pigs into diabetic monkeys and found that such immature islets were more capable of multiplying and growing—and possibly less likely to trigger an immune response.

These promising results have now been confirmed by investigators at the University of Pittsburgh. A group in Israel also used embryonic pig pancreases. A variety of other techniques for preventing rejection of transplanted pig islets have been reported in other animal studies. Pig islets have also been transplanted into baboons and other nonhuman primates, per reports from Australia and several other institutions.

Attempts have been made to encapsulate islets, thereby minimizing or possibly eliminating the need for immunosuppressive drugs. However, this strategy, in the hands of various independent research groups that have transplanted pig islets into nonhuman primates, has not yet resulted in prolonged restoration of insulin independence or in tight blood glucose control. Because of the unique features of cell xenografts, such as pig islets, it is possible that immunosuppressive protocols could be quite similar to those in transplants between similar species. Hering's group, again, showed that cultured islets from pigs transplanted into diabetic monkeys restored blood glucose control consistently for more than 100 days. In one of their subgroups, all 5 of the monkeys survived at least 68 days posttransplant; 4 of them survived 111 or more days. The longest survival time was 187 days; that monkey was sacrificed for further evaluation of the islets, which were still fully functioning.

A key goal for solving the islet supply problem was to develop a method of raising pathogen-free pigs, a goal that was accomplished by Hering's group in collaboration with the Spring Point Project. The mission of the Spring Point Project, a nonprofit Minnesota corporation established in 2004, is to expedite widespread availability of high-quality pig islet tissue for patients with diabetes. The donor pigs are raised in biosecure barrier facilities under carefully controlled conditions to ensure the absence of microorganisms (bacteria, fungi, and viruses) known to have the potential to infect humans. So-called porcine endogenous retroviruses (PERVs), however, cannot be removed from donor pigs, because PERVs are integrated in the genome of all pigs. Nevertheless, productive PERV infections have never been observed in either animals or humans exposed to pig tissue. The theoretical threat to human recipients of pig islet xenografts has recently been further reduced by identifying pigs that cannot transmit PERVs to human cells. In 2008, the U.S. Food and Drug Administration (FDA) agreed that pigs born of parents delivered by cesarean section in a barrier facility, after 2 generations, can serve as donor pigs for the planned clinical trial.

In 2006, Henk-Jan Schuurman, an experienced xenotransplant researcher and CEO of the Spring Point Project, and Dr. Michael Martin, a well-recognized expert in advanced swine reproduction technologies, introduced piglets delivered by cesarean section into the Spring Point Project. By the end of 2009, the partnership between the Spring Point Project and the Schulze Diabetes Institute at the University of Minnesota anticipates submitting an investigational new drug application to the FDA.

Clinical evaluation of pig islets in Phase II and III trials, which are anticipated to begin in 2010, in people with type 1 diabetes will take about 5 years. By the end of 2015, assuming that the clinical trials yield positive results, a biologics license application will be submitted to the FDA.

If all goes according to plan, a 21,000-square-foot biosecure building at the Spring Point Project site will be home to about 100 "medical grade" pigs. Very few buildings of this kind exist in the world. Pancreatic islet cells from those pathogen-free pigs will be transplanted into diabetic patients enrolled in the clinical trials. The tantalizing possibility is that, within the next 10 to 20 years, many diabetic patients might be cured. Currently, in the United States alone, 1.5 million people have type 1 diabetes and another 20 million have type 2 diabetes.

Pig islets are only the beginning. If the clinical trials are successful, these pathogen-free pigs could also then serve as a source of other organs for transplants a well. The liver, kidney, pancreas, heart, lungs, and possibly brain could then become available to meet the demands of further development of the miracle of the 20th century, namely, successful solid organ transplantation.

STEM CELLS?

Besides animals, another possible future source of grafts for transplants would be stem cells. But unfortunately, stem cells may have many drawbacks, such as the development of tumors in recipients. Nonetheless, as stem cell research progresses and is refined, stem cells may well be a source at least of islet cells. What exactly are stem cells? Would their use for transplants be controversial?

The term "stem cells" was first proposed in 1908, referring to cells that would eventually differentiate into blood elements (such as red blood cells, white blood cells, and platelets). Two main categories of stem cells are now recognized: those derived from **embryos** and those derived from **adult somatic** cells (the soma is body tissue, as distinguished from germ cells).

Embryonic stem cells are pluripotent, which means that they can develop into every cell, every tissue, and every organ in the human body. They were first isolated from mice in 1981. The first human embryonic stem cell line was developed by a group of investigators at the University of Wisconsin in Madison in 1998. In 2001, then-president George W. Bush said he would allow research using existing embryonic cell lines, but, for what he called ethical reasons, would not fund research on the creation of additional cell lines. However, a variety of advocates of the potential that stem cells might represent kept clamoring for an end to Bush's policy. In March 2009, President Barack Obama overturned Bush's rules. For the first time, federal dollars can now support research that eventually will rely on ongoing destruction of discarded embryos.

Embryonic stem cells are the building blocks of the human body. The stem cells inside of the embryo will eventually give rise to every cell, tissue, and organ in the fetus's body. Unlike other cells, they can replicate to create more of their own kind of cell. When a stem cell divides, it can make any of the 220 different types of cells in the human body. Stem cells also have the capability of self-renewal.

In contrast to embryonic stem cells, adult stem cells (also known as somatic cells) are specific to a particular organ or tissue. For example, separate adult stem cells give rise to the heart, the brain, the bone marrow (blood), and the liver. Adult stem cells are built-in repair kits, regenerating cells damaged by disease, injury, and everyday wear and tear. Previously, adult stem cells were believed to be more limited than embryonic stem cells and to only give rise to the same type of tissue from which they originated. But new research suggests that adult stem cells may have the potential to generate other types of cells as well. For example, liver cells might be coaxed to produce insulin, which normally would be made by the pancreas. This capability is known as plasticity or transdifferentiation.

In the laboratory, embryonic stem cells can be isolated from the blastocyst (a mass of 50 to 100 cells that, in humans, is about 4 to 5 days old; in other words, an early-stage embryo). Embryonic stem cells are part of the inner cells of the blastocyst. In contrast, adult stem cells are much harder for scientists to work with, because they are more difficult to extract and culture than their embryonic counterparts. In adult tissue, stem cells are hard to find. Moreover, scientists have difficulty in getting adult stem cells to replicate (or self-renew) in the laboratory. Scientists do know that turning genes on and off is crucial to the process of differentiation. So they have been experimenting by inserting certain genes into the culture of adult stem cells and then using those genes to coax stem cells to turn into specific types of cells. But some sort of signal is needed to actually trigger the adult stem cells to differentiate. Scientists are still searching for that signal.

Stem cells (either embryonic or adult) could be used to repair cells and tissues that have been damaged by disease or injury. Such treatment is known as cell-based therapy. One potential application is to inject embryonic stem cells (or cardiac cells made from embryonic stem cells) into a patient's heart to repair cells that have been damaged by a heart attack. In a Mayo Clinic study, researchers induced a heart attack in rats and then injected embryonic stem cells from other rodents into the rats' damaged hearts; eventually, the embryonic stem cells regenerated the damaged muscle tissue and even improved the rats' heart function.

Embryonic or adult stem cells may also one day be used to repair brain cells in patients with Parkinson's disease. Such patients lack the chemical messenger dopamine. Without dopamine, their movements become jerky and uncoordinated, and they suffer from uncontrollable tremors. Researchers who injected rodent embryonic stem cells into the brains of rats with Parkinson's disease found that the stem cells regenerated dopamine-producing nerve cells, improving the rats' condition. Scientists hope that one day they can replicate this success in human patients. Actor Michael J. Fox is a vocal proponent of this research; his foundation has donated more than $35 million to help fund Parkinson's research.

The most likely afflictions that may one day be treated with cell-based therapy are Parkinson's disease, diabetes, heart disease, cancer, spinal cord injury, burns, Alzheimer's, and vision loss.

Perhaps the biggest hope is expressed by individuals with spinal cord damage that resulted in paraplegia or quadriplegia. In a 2005 study, partially paralyzed rats could walk after embryonic stem cells were administered into the spinal cord area of damage, thereby producing myelin so that nerve signals can pass. Indeed, based in part on that study, the first clinical trial using cells derived from human embryonic stem cells has now been approved by the FDA to treat patients with spinal cord injury. Such promising advances must be greeted with cautious optimism. The Christopher and Dana Reeve Foundation is constantly trying to balance the hope against the hype. Currently, more than 400,000 people have chronic spinal cord injuries, with 12,000 new cases each year. For myelin-restoring therapy to work, the spinal cord injury must be under 14 days' duration. So far, the likelihood of getting such treatment so quickly seems remote. Investigators in this area have stated that "no one is going to be cured any time soon."

Of the numerous conditions that may one day be treated successfully with cell-based therapy, I feel that Parkinson's disease (with programmed cells making dopamine) and diabetes (with programmed cells making insulin) are 2 of the most likely.

Heart disease might be another, but controversy continues regarding the advisability of injecting cells from bone marrow directly into the heart or into the coronary vessels serving the blood supply to the heart. Nancy Reagan remains a strong advocate of stem cell research, primarily to treat Alzheimer's disease, which had stricken and eventually killed her husband, former president Ronald Reagan. Yet the likelihood of successfully treating Alzheimer's with cell-based therapy seems low, to me, since it results from large deposits of a protein called amyloid that form plaques in the brain. The plaques interfere with transmission of neural messages in the brain and result in the death of brain cells involved in memory.

An abiding concern is whether or not foreign stem cells (embryonic or adult) would trigger a rejection process in recipients of cell-based therapy. Even in the long-established field of solid-organ transplantation, we have not accomplished immunologic tolerance to grafts; immunosuppressive drugs are necessary, except in recipients whose donor is their identical twin. I feel that the ideal research, at the present time, involves reprogramming adult cells into stem cells. If individuals' own cells could be converted into stem cells, the use of immunosuppressive drugs (and the associated complications and problems) would be unnecessary.

Diabetic patients, in my view, will be the first beneficiaries of both xenotransplants (involving pig organs) and cell-based therapy (involving embryonic or adult stem cells). With curing diabetes as a beginning, I hope that within the next 10 to 20 years, many of the other dreams of these 2 frontiers will be realized.

References

(1) Akcam T. A Shameful Act: The Armenian Genocide and the Question of Turkish Responsibility. New York: Holt Paperbacks, Henry Holt and Company, LLC, 2006.

(2) Küss R, Teinturier J, and Milliez P. Quelques essays de greffe du rein chez l'homme. Mémories Académie de Chirurgie 77: 22-23, 755-768, 1951.

(3) Harper HA, Najarian JS, and Silen W. Effect of intravenously administered amino acids on blood ammonia. Proc Soc Exp Biol Med 92: 558-560, 1956.

(4) Najarian JS and McCorkle HJ. Experimental grafting of a suspension of skin particles. Surg Forum VII: 125-129, 1957 (October).

(5) Najarian JS, Murray DH, Buster CD, and Grimes OF. Utilization of the ileocecal valve as a substitute for the "cardioesophageal sphincter." Surg Forum VII: 344-348, 1957 (October).

(6) Murray DH, Najarian JS, Buster CD, Scott KG, Harper HA, and McCorkle HJ. Absorption of radioactive iron after gastrectomy. Surg Forum VIII: 2211-214, 1958 (October).

(7) Najarian JS, Hine DE, Whitock RM, and McCorkle HJ. Effect of pancreatic secretions on the gallbladder. Arch Surg 74: 6: 890-899, 1957 (June).

(8) Najarian JS and Feldman JD. Passive transfer of tuberculin sensitivity by tritiated thymidine-labeled lymphoid cells. J Exp Med 114: 5: 779-790, 1961 (November).

(9) Najarian JS and Feldman JD. Passive transfer of transplantation immunity. I. Tritiated lymphoid cells. II. Lymphoid cells in Millipore chambers. J Exp Med 115: 5: 1083-1093, 1962 (May).

(10) Najarian JS and Gulyassy PF. Current status of renal homotransplantations. J Calif Med 107: 2: 129-140, 1967 (August).

(11) Najarian JS, Gulyassy PF, Duffy G, Stoney RJ, and Braunstein P. Protection of the donor kidney during homotransplantations. Ann Surg 164: 3: 398-417, 1966 (September).

(12) Belzer FO, Ashby BC, and Dunphy JE. 24-hour and 72-hour preservation of canine kidneys. Lancet 2: 536, 1967.

(13) Collins GM, Bravo-Shugarman M, and Terasaki PI. Kidney preservation for transportation. Initial perfusion and 30 hours ice storage. Lancet 2: 1219, 1969.

(14) Payne R, Perkins HA, and Najarian JS. Compatibility for seven leukocyte antigens in renal homografts: Utilization of a microagglutination test with few sera. In Curtoni ES, Mattuiz PL, and Tosi RM (eds): Histocompatibility Testing. Denmark: RJ Schmidt, Vogens, 1967, pp. 237-245.

(15) Cochrum KC, Okimoto JT, and Najarian JS. Experimental thoracic duct shunt. J Appl Physiol 24: 2: 247-248, 1968 (February).

(16) Perper RJ, Okimoto JT, Cochrum KC, Ramsey H, and Najarian JS. A rapid method for purification of large quantities of antilymphocytic serum. Proc Soc Exp Biol Med 125: 2: 575-580, 1967 (June).

(17) Perper RJ and Najarian JS. Experimental renal heterotransplantation. I. In widely divergent species. Transplantation 4: 4: 377-388, 1966 (July).

(18) Perper RJ and Najarian JS. Experimental renal heterotransplantation. II. In closely related species. Transplantation 4: 6: 700-712, 1966 (November).

(19) Perper RJ and Najarian JS. Experimental renal heterotransplantation. III. Passive transfer of transplantation immunity. Transplantation 5: 3: 514-533, 1967 (May).

(20) Reemtsma K, McCracken BH, Schlegel JU, et al. Renal heterotransplantation in man. Ann Surg 160: 384, 1964.

(21) Hering BJ, Wijkstrom M, Graham ML, et al. Prolonged diabetes reversal after intraportal xenotransplantation of wild-type porcine islets in immunosuppressed nonhuman primates. Nature Medicine 12: 3, 2006 (March).

(22) Strickland T and Strickland S. The Markle Scholars: A Brief History. New York: Prodist, 1976.

(23) Wilson LG. Medical Revolution in Minnesota: A History of the University of Minnesota Medical School. St. Paul: Midewiwin Press, 1978.

(24) Lazarow A, Wells LJ, Carpenter AM, et al. Islet differentiation, orang culture, and transplantation. Diabetes 22: 413-428, 1973.

(25) Najarian JS. Presidential Address: The Making of the Transplantation Society. The Transplantation Society Bulletin 5: 8-13, 1996 (December).

(26) Ryan EA, Paty BW, Senior PA, et al. Five-year follow-up after clinical islet transplantation. Diabetes 54: 2060-2069, 2005.

(27) Gruessner RWG, Sutherland DER. Transplantation of the Pancreas. New York: Springer-Verlag, 2004.

(28) Bliss M. The Discovery of Insulin. Chicago: University of Chicago Press, 1982.

(29) Herdman RC and Najarian JS. Southern Medical Journal 61: 8: 894-896, 1968 (August).

(30) Humphrey HH. Late A Senator From Minnesota, Memorial Addresses Delivered in Congress. Memorial Addresses Delivered in the 95th Congress, 2nd Session. Senate Document, No. 95-105, U.S. Government Printing Office, Washington, 1978.

(31) Brokaw T. Tom Brokaw speaks to the American Surgical Association: Excerpts from An Anchorman Looks at the World. The Cutting Edge. University of Minnesota Surgery Department Newsletter, pp. 1-7, 10-11, 1989 (August).

(32) Najarian JS. Presidential Address: The Skill, Science, and Soul of the Surgeon. Annals of Surgery 210: 3: 257-267, 1989 (September).

(33) Woodruff MFA and Anderson NF. Effect of lymphocyte depletion by thoracic duct fistula and administration of antilymphocyte serum on the survival of skin homografts in rats. Nature 200: 702, 1963.

(34) Starzl TE, Marchioro TL, Porter KA, Iwasaki Y, and Cerilli CJ. The use of heterologous antilymphoid agents in canine renal and liver homotransplantations and in human renal transplantation. Surgery, Gynecology, and Obstetrics 124: 301-18, 1967.

(35) Najarian JS, Merkel FK, Moore GE, Good RA, and Aust JC. Clinical use of antilymphoblast serum. Transplant Proc 1: 1: 460-462, 1969 (March).

(36) Najarian JS, Simmons RL, Moberg AW, Gewurz H, Merkel FK, and Moore GE. Antiserum to cultured human lymphoblasts. Ann Surg 170: 4: 617-629, 1969 (October).

(37) Gewurz H, Moberg AW, Simmons RL, Pollara B, Gunnarsson A, Soll R, and Najarian JS. Induction of immunologic tolerance to ALG in man. Surg Forum XX: 259-261, 1969 (October).

(38) Najarian JS, Simmons RL, Condie RM, Thompson EJ, Fryd DS, Howard RJ, Matas AJ, Sutherland DER, Ferguson RM, and Schmidtke JR. Seven years' experience with antilymphoblast globulin for renal transplantation from cadaver donors. Ann Surg 184: 3: 352-367, 1976 (September).

(39) Halloran PF, Lien J, Aprile M, White N. Preliminary results of a randomized comparison of cyclosporine and Minnesota antilymphoblast globulin. Transplantation Proc 14: 4: 627-30, 1982 (December).

(40) Halloran, PF, Aprile MA, Farewell V, Ludwin D, Smith EK, Tsai SY, Bear RA, Cole EH, Fenton SS, Cattran DC. Early function as the principal correlate of graft survival. A multivariate analysis of 200 cadaveric renal transplants treated with a protocol incorporating antilymphocyte globulin and cyclosporine. Transplantation 46: 2: 223-8, 1988 (August).

(41) Sutherland DER, Goetz FC, Chinn PL, Elick BA, Simmons RL, and Najarian JS. Pancreas transplantation at the University of Minnesota: Experience with 68 recent cases. In Pozza G et al (eds): Diet, Diabetes, and Atherosclerosis. New York: Raven Press, 1984, pp. 89-94.

(42) Lundquist JW. United States v Najarian: A postmortem on regulatory misdirection. Archives of Surgery 131: 9: 911-14, 1996 (September).